ETHICAL ISSUES IN THE 21ST CENTURY

# INTERNATIONAL PERSPECTIVES OF MULTICULTURALISM

## THE ETHICAL CHALLENGES

# ETHICAL ISSUES IN THE 21ST CENTURY

Additional books in this series can be found on Nova's website under the Series tab.

Additional e-books in this series can be found on Nova's website under the e-book tab.

ETHICAL ISSUES IN THE 21ST CENTURY

# INTERNATIONAL PERSPECTIVES OF MULTICULTURALISM

## THE ETHICAL CHALLENGES


ORNETTE D. CLENNON
EDITOR



nova publishers
*New York*

## Library of Congress Cataloging-in-Publication Data

ISBN: 978-1-63483-971-6
Names: Clennon, Ornette D., 1969- editor.
Title: International perspectives of multiculturalism. the ethical
challenges / editor, Ornette D. Clennon.
Description: Hauppauge, New York. Nova Science Publishers, Inc., [2015] |
Series: Ethical issues in the 21st century | Includes bibliographical
references and index.
Identifiers: LCCN 2015038874 | ISBN 9781634839716 (hardcover)
Subjects: LCSH: Multiculturalism. | Ethnic relations.
Classification: LCC HM1271.I5888 2015 | DDC 305.8--dc23 LC record available at
http://lccn.loc.gov/2015038874

*Published by Nova Science Publishers, Inc. † New York*

# CONTENTS

# PREFACE

We seem to be living in an era where identity and belonging are crucial political ideologies that have become matters of life and death for many everyday-people around the world. These days with social media, we are witnessing the global effects of these ideologies, as they unfold with huge humanitarian crises, in part, caused by large numbers of refugees and migrants fleeing war and persecution in their own countries. However, more worryingly, we are also witnessing how the traditionally safe havens of refuge in the Global North seem to be struggling to muster the common political will to welcome these often desperate people in to their countries, with all too frequent tragic consequences. However, we do not even need to look at the huge numbers of geographically displaced peoples around the world to bear another witness to a quiet humanitarian crisis that is one of cultural displacement. Movements such as #BlackLivesMatters are helping us to confront this growing phenomenon of internal ostracisation, disenfranchisement and displacement, as an increasing number of communities around the world are beginning to feel like "Outcasts on the Inside" of their own homelands. Now more than ever, perhaps using 'multiculturalism' as an important conceptual tool, we need to make a concerted effort to understand the roles of belonging, stakeholdership and identity in the fight for social justice. We also need to take an honest look at our global histories (memories) in order to understand why we are where we are, at present and what we can do to shape our futures for the better.

Ornette D Clennon, Editor

# ACKNOWLEDGMENTS

**Ornette D Clennon:** I would like to thank God without whom none of this would be possible. I would like to thank Shaun Connell (book cover photograph; *Flags, Whistles & Horns*) and Faye Bruce (Critical Race and Ethnicity Research Cluster, Manchester Metropolitan University) for the stimulating conversations that made large parts of my contribution to this volume possible. I would like to thank Henry Ngawoofah (Making Education a Priority, MEaP) and Blue Matthews-Mason (C.L.R. James Community Trust) for their unflinching community support. I would also like to thank Professors Rebecca Lawthom and Carolyn Kagan (Manchester Metropolitan University, UK), Dr. Robbie Shilliam (Queen Mary University of London, UK), Dr. Claudia Sampaio (Federal University of the Amazon, Brazil) and Dr. Deborah Gabriel (Bournemouth University, UK and Black British Academics) for their amazing academic support and solidarity. And finally, I would like to thank all of my fellow contributors for making this such a fascinating volume!

**Jeong-Ae Park:** I would like to thank Jan Jagodzinski at University of Alberta, Canada.

# NOTES ABOUT CONTRIBUTORS

### Ornette D. Clennon (Editor)

*Dr. Ornette D. Clennon* is a Visiting Enterprise Fellow at Manchester Metropolitan University, UK. Ornette writes for Media Diversified and Open Democracy and is a Public Engagement Ambassador for the National Co-ordinating Centre for Public Engagement (NCCPE). He is also a community activist at local and national levels and works with the C.L.R. James Community Trust, Making Education a Priority (MEaP), Black British Academics and the National Resource Centre for Supplementary Education. Ornette's enterprise and activism work has been recognised with the 2011 NCCPE Beacons New Partnerships Award. Ornette is widely published and his previous books include *Alternative Education and Community Engagement: Making Education a Priority* (2014) and *Urban Dialectics, The Market and Youth Engagement: The Black Face of Eurocentrism?* (2015).

### Jeong-Ae Park

*Jeong-Ae Park* is a professor of Art Education at Gongju National University of Education. She studied art and art history in Korea where she gained a BFA and MA from Hongik University, Seoul and studied in the UK where she received her PhD from University of Surrey. Her research interests are in the relationships of curriculum to contemporary art and culture. She has published over 30 papers and has edited *Art Education as Critical Cultural Inquiry*, and written two books: *Postmodern Art and Art Education* (2001), and *A New Paradigm for Art Education: Art as Meaning Making* (2008) which was recognised as a 2009 Excellent Academic Publication by the Ministry of Culture and Sports and Tourism of Korea. Currently she serves on editorial board of *Journal of Research in Art Education* (Korean Society for Education through Art) and *International Journal of Education through Art* (InSEA).

**Narciso Leandro Xavier Baez**

*Narciso Leandro Xavier Baez* is a Federal Judge in Brazil, since 1996, scholar and commentator specialising in international human rights law and constitutional law. He is Director of the Centre for Excellence in Law and a Professor and Researcher from the Universidade do Oeste de Santa Catarina, Brazil (UNOESC).

**Mahama Tawat**

*Mahama Tawat* is an Assistant professor of Public Policy and Administration and a Research Fellow at the Centre for Advanced Studies of the Higher School of Economics, Moscow. He is also a Research Affiliate at the Malmö Institute for the Study of Migration, Diversity and Welfare, Malmö University, Sweden. He graduated from the University of Otago in New Zealand and the Universities of Stockholm and Dalarna in Sweden.

His research centres on migration policy in Scandinavia and in a comparative perspective and public management reforms. He has published in such journals as the International Journal of Cultural Policy.

# INTRODUCTION
## WHY SHOULD WE CARE?

*Ornette D. Clennon**
**Manchester Metropolitan University, Manchester, UK**

Even though this volume does not directly discuss movements like #BlackLivesMatters or the current refugee crisis in Europe, the chapters in their own ways shed a little light on some of the underpinning cultural and psychopolitical dimensions to these crises. Thinking about what multiculturalism is and how it can be used to help us think about the way in which people are citizenised is very important for looking at the social justice issues underpinning our global humanitarian crises. However, also thinking about how these citizenisation processes are being globalised and what their driving impulses are, also throws up some interesting questions, in Chapter 4.

In Chapter 1, Mahama Tawat offers us a firm foundation for envisioning the various processes of citizenisation. I was intrigued by the initial idea that enforced assimilation was intended to act as a 'melting pot' where everyone could be bound together by an abstract notion of nationhood at the expense of their (indigenous) cultural backgrounds. This for me, very much resonated with Chapter 2's take on stakeholdership because what was assumed with assimilation was that the binding nature of civic unity waste be found in a synthetic re-telling of a history, or false memory of what the nation would like to be, not what it actually is. It is as though reaching out to its Lacanian mirror

* E-mail: o.clennon@mmu.ac.uk.

reflection (in Chapter 4), the nation is troubled by its fragmented populous, so identifies with its imago or ideal image of itself (enforced civic unity).

This means that this false memory or cultural memory has to suppress the individual history of its citizens in order to survive (like the market in Chapter 4). So, in Chapter 2, Ornette Clennon asks questions around Chapter 1's 'intentionality' of its citizens. Chapter 1 explains that this flattening out effect of the 'melting pot' meant that official stories or identities of difference, ethnic or otherwise did not feature very highly in the French Republicanist version of assimilation. So in effect, because the back history of the individual was not important for determining citizenship, the individual's intention became the key factor. Would they learn the language of their nation? Would they take up arms to defend their nation? In other words, what would an individual need to do to prove her loyalty to her country? This question is redolent of the 'Politics of Respectability' (Chapter 2) where the individual is forced to live in a simulated reality created by the dominant group in order to prove their worth. Narciso Leandro Xavier Baez in Chapter 3 describes this as an act of objectification where the individual in effect loses their autonomy; an autonomy that is supposed to guarantee their Human Rights to 'human dignity'. Seen in this light, much political multiculturalism, that is, the political implementation of ideological multicultural values can be seen as potentially being in conflict with one's 'human dignity' as embodied by their autonomy.

However, Chapter 2 turns this question on its head by asking whether the individual's history has already qualified her for citizenship and already implies her loyalty. This is an especially interesting question for post-colonial immigrants living in the Mother Country of their former colonial homelands because it can be argued, as Chapter 2 does, that the post-colonial groups are already embedded in their Mother country's history so should not need to prove their 'intentionality'. So the question now becomes, why have the histories of the post-colonial groups been forgotten? And instead of contemplating the 'intentionality' of the individual, we should be examining the 'intentionality' of the state.

Even if we take into consideration Chapter 1's Liberal Nationalism, which seems to be a more relaxed version of assimilation where non-majoritarian cultural backgrounds are given more leeway to officially exist (albeit privately), all we still seem to be talking about is to what degree the state can do their citizens a favour by recognising their cultural backgrounds (entitlements). If this is the case for post-colonial groups, Chapter 2 recognises that this puts them in a very odd predicament of having to ask the state (that they historically helped to build) to grant them the favour of recognition and tolerance. This discourse is summarised in Chapter 2 with the concept of stakeholdership, as mentioned earlier. Within this concept it is assumed that the pluralist universalism that Bhikhu Parekh talks about where individuals need to feel belonging and acceptance cannot really happen unless the citizens' a priori belonging or stake in the nation has been recognised. Charles Taylor's 'politics of recognition' touches on this aspect of stakeholdership for indigenous people, as the example of New Zealand's Treaty of Waitangi demonstrates (to a degree). As an aside, I thought that Iris Marion Young's 'politics of difference' or idea of "differentiated citizenship" slightly reminded me of an updated version of UK 3S's Multiculturalism discussed in Chapter 2 in the guise of Equality and Diversity strategies. Here, I was troubled by the equating of socially marginalised groups (such as the elderly, lesbians, gay men, bisexuals and transgendered people (LGBT) and women) with culturally marginalised groups such as immigrants or post-colonial and indigenous groups. Whereas I believe that social justice is important for all, this "differentiated citizenship" idea reminded me the 1980's New Public Management's tendency to deprioritise matters around race. I strongly believe that the a priori stakeholdership of, for example, white elderly people, white LBGT and white women is not in question. The citizenisation processes of these white groups are not in question because it is already assumed that they are inherently fully paid up members of their nation and have an assumed national stake in the nation's cultural memory. There will undoubtedly be important issues around social justice that still need to be addressed for these groups but to equate their struggle to the struggles around race, which underpins all other areas of social justice is to ignore the distinct cultural histories of each of these marginalised groups.

*Why is this so important and why can't all marginalised people unite against social justice?*

While I think that it is, indeed, important for all marginalised groups to unite and fight social injustices, I think that it is equally important to literally take Young's 'politics of difference' at her word. It is crucial to distinguish between the cultural histories of each marginalised group in terms of how it is marginalised and subjected to social injustice, in order to execute the appropriate strategies of resistance. Lumping all the marginalised groups into an undifferentiated mass of the oppressed, encourages the formation of a 'hierarchy of the oppressed'.[1] It needs to be acknowledged that not all marginalised groups suffer the same levels of oppression. In fact, some marginalised groups actually receive social privileges that other groups do not. I am particularly reminded of W.E.B. Du Bois' term 'psychological wage' that he coined in the 1930's to describe how the poor white working class American still was able to expect better treatment from society than their black counterpart, despite the extreme hardships they both faced. So, this potentially unthinking aggregation of the oppressed can actually lead to greater oppression within what could become a hidden 'hierarchy of oppression'. Another reason why Young's idea of widening the concept of culture to include social groupings worries me is that in these alliances, the issue around intersectionality tends not be considered. For example within the wider LGBT movement, black LGBTs still suffer racism and societal "othering" from their fellow marginalised white LGBT peers. This form of 'inter-marginal' oppression is even more apparent and theorised in Black Feminism by the likes of Patricia Hill Collins.

*So why does all of this remind me of Equalities and Diversity statements and strategies?*

Well, in not acknowledging the need for specific strategies to resist specific forms of oppression with specific histories, nothing is done other than to monitor representation. Chapter 2 makes a joke by saying that the carnivalesque spectacle of the saris, samosas and steel bands (the 3S's) has been replaced by a carnivalesque spectacle of pie charts, bar graphs and tables indicating the representation or lack of the whole rainbow of marginalised groups without the implementation of any structural changes as a consequence.

However, what was really intriguing for me was how all these ideological forms of multiculturalism i.e., assimilation, liberal nationalism, 'politics of recognition', 'politics of difference' and pluralist universalism all seemed to meet at a point of a liberal minimum. This is a concept that proposes a notional minimum cultural competency that an immigrant is expected to have (in terms of managing their cultural practices). So, cultural practices such as forced marriages and female genital mutilation (FGM) are deemed illiberal and unacceptable, whereas wearing a veil can be ideologically tolerated, if not

[1] I am not entirely sure Young is advocating this to be fair but this approach tends to lead to this result.

wholly accepted. Bhikhu Parekh makes this anomaly even starker by suggesting that although all cultures have worth and need to be respected, not all cultures are equal in receiving such worthiness or respect. This reminds me of my instinctive suspicion of Young's 'politics of difference' and the creation of potential hierarchies of oppression.

*But more profoundly, this made me ask, well, who actually gets to decide these values of worthiness and who decides this liberal minimum (especially as the marginalised are not at the decision making tables)?*

Chapter 4 looks at trying to answer this question. Ornette Clennon examines the phenomenon of 'whiteness' (and its disavowed opposite, 'blackness') and unpicks its tenacious hold on its subjects. This chapter looks at this near-invisible psychopathological structure of domination to which earlier chapters' talk of majoritarian culture alludes. This feature of dominance is a leitmotif, which runs throughout the volume and Chapter 4 tries to look at the psychological structures that make it possible to exist. This assimilationist idea from Chapter 1 of making citizens of individuals not groups returns rebooted in a very twenty first century marketised version. In trying to explain what Globalisation's "unique endowments" are (to coin a phrase from Edward Said) and why they seem to leave the same imprint on all cultures they touch, the chapter traces the processes by which 'whiteness' comes into being and transforms itself into a market derivative of individuality (market freedom). Through its market transformation 'whiteness' decouples its racial locus to become a template for social relationships within the market. So, we begin to see the emergence of 'proximities to whiteness' that again talk to the inter-marginal hierarchies of oppression.

Finally as a soothing and redemptive antidote to the psychopathological discourse of dominance and mastery, Chapter 5 illustrates how a group of Korean artists regained their Koreanness on their own terms without the need to master the "Other." I was particularly intrigued by Jeong-Ae Park's perspective of non-Koreanness (or the white mainstream) as being the "Other" rather than the usual Orientalist positioning. This means that Chapter 5 very subtly explores the idea of the rhizome as transverse roots growing and rooting in reaction to their relationship to the "Other" in order to find new ways of being, which exists ambiguously between Koreanness and "Otherness" in a liminal space. Chapter 5 completes the cycle of dialecticism (initiated by Charles Taylor in Chapter 1) where for Park, 'being' cannot exist in isolation but can only exist as a result of interaction. Chapter 5's gently unfolding exploration of interaction and being, offers a real antidote to the neoliberal isolationism that is globally marketised as the Lacanian imago to which we are told to aspire.

*So how does all of this relate to the real world humanitarian crises of cultural as well as geographical displacement that we see around us today?*

By making visible the routinely invisible, this volume highlights some of the ways that power is executed and marginalises specific groups of people.

By helping us to realise the importance of cultural memory (both national and ethnic).

By helping us to think in a multi-layered (intersectional) way when resisting social injustices but by first helping us to see social injustices in a multi-layered way, too.

By helping us to remember that we always have choices even if we are told that we don't or more perversely but perhaps more importantly, that we don't always have the range of choices that we are led to believe. Here, of course, I am alluding to Pierre Bourdieu's misrecognition but only to emphasise that once we open our eyes to the latter, we indeed can make other choices that have not been necessarily offered to us.

And finally,

By helping us to remember that all of these ethical considerations have real political consequences, which as citizens we can act on to make the changes we want and need.

In: International Perspectives of Multiculturalism ISBN: 978-1-63483-971-6
Editor: Ornette D. Clennon 

*Chapter 1*

# THE ETHICS OF MULTICULTURALISM: A REAPPRAISAL

***Mahama Tawat****
Centre of Advanced Studies,
Higher School of Economics, Russia

## ABSTRACT

There is much disagreement among scholars about the concepts of multiculturalism and assimilation. As a consequence, they are polysemic and in need of both differentiation and homogenisation. In this chapter, Mahama Tawat will seek to differentiate between the ethical considerations of Assimilation, Liberal Nationalism and Multiculturalism by examining the theoretical frameworks proposed by David Miller and the various readings of the 'Celebration of Difference' as advocated by Charles Taylor, Iris Marion Young and Bhikhu Parekh.

**Keywords:** multiculturalism, assimilation, group rights, uniformisation, liberal nationalism

---

* Email: mahama.tawat@otago.ac.nz.

# Introduction

Unlike the 'politics of control' that deal with the process behind the admission of foreigners into a country, the 'politics of incorporation' examine the sociopolitical and cultural integration of immigrants into the society and their relationship with issues such as citizenship and national identity [1]. Assimilation and multiculturalism are the two most recurrent theories but they are also the object of enormous contention among scholars; mainly because there is such a proliferation of concepts [2]. Assimilation is the oldest and default form of cultural policy towards foreigners. Enforced assimilation, as practised in the early days of European colonisation, compelled indigenous peoples to abandon their cultures and adopt the cultures of the dominant group. This often meant that they were treated as second class citizens. However, it was superseded by non-coercive assimilation in the post-war (WW2) era. It is argued that non-coercive assimilation is mainly characterised by the promotion of the national culture but the acceptance of other cultural practices as long as they are kept in the private sphere. This is illustrated by its two main strands, French Republicanism [3] and liberal nationalism whose most influential representative is David Miller [4].

Multiculturalism internationally emerged in the mid-1960s and 1970s as a result of both the Canadian government's handling of grievances aired by the nationalists from Quebec and the changes in immigration laws in Australia [5]. In general, advocates of multiculturalism promote both the recognition of all cultural identities within a territorial unit and some form of collective rights. The main element of multiculturalism is the 'celebration of difference'. I will later examine how this 'celebration of difference' is interpreted differently by Charles Taylor's 'Politics of Recognition', Iris Marion Young's 'Politics of Difference' and Bhikhu Parekh's 'Pluralist Universalism'.

# Theories of Assimilation

## French Republicanism

Enforced assimilation, the earliest and most radical form of assimilation, was the goal of many European states' cultural policy during early colonial times with respect to Native Americans in the USA, Aboriginals in Australia, First Nations in Canada and the Māori in New Zealand [6] this also included national minorities such as the Saami in Sweden and the Inuit in Denmark. At that time, indigenous cultures were deemed abhorrent and inferior so it was felt that they had to be uprooted and re-moulded in order to benefit from the so-called more advanced and civilised European and Christian cultures [7]. With independence in colonial territories and the end of white-only immigration policies, enforced assimilation was abandoned; leaving space for the only other existing form of assimilation, French Republicanism.

French Republicanism is based on the concept of the melting pot; the idea of developing a single national culture by blending all particularisms into a single national identity [8]. Uniformity is seen as the means of achieving equality and cohesion. Historian Jules Michelet (1798-1874), its mastermind in the wake of the French revolution of 1789, conceived and propagated the notion of France as a melting pot where all the French sub-national identities would melt into a single French cultural identity [9]. Originally, Michelet [10] conceived the nation itself in his *Tableaux de la France* as the mechanism of assimilation, “a nourishing and assimilating land” [11] (p. 44) that shaped the identity of its people [12]. Pierre Vidal de la Blache [13], a prominent geographer, explained that Germanness is essentially an ethnic idea for Germans whereas the French see their Frenchness as bound to the French soil and their recollected pleasure of living on it. However, with the advent of the Third Republic in 1870, the French state became the agent of cultural reproduction through four main mechanisms: public education, the French language, the army and centralisation [14, 15].

The first mechanism, public education was enforced by the Jules Ferry Laws of 1883, which required public education to teach (indoctrinate) republican values such as citizenship and patriotism [16]. Jules Ferry (1832-1893) after whom the Laws were named was a prominent Education Minister and one of the main advocates of French colonial expansion. He implemented the laws through the establishment of free and compulsory schools, state control and the secularisation of the school curriculum. For example, he created a newsletter and sent it to school teachers that was called “Lettres aux instituteurs” (Letters to school teachers) in which he distilled his pedagogic guidelines [17]. He banned religious education in public schools, so the state itself became “laïc” or secular and promoted patriotic history books such as that of Ernest Lavisse’s eighteen volume history of France that were read by about fifteen million French children between 1880 and 1914 [18]. The 1989 “foulard affair” in which three French Muslim pupils wearing headscarves were excluded from a school on the grounds of “laicité” or secularism epitomises this principle [19]. Although the overwhelming majority of French citizens are Catholic, the country does not give any official or public status to the Catholic Church in contrast to England where the Anglican Church is still the state church and the monarchy has to be Anglican.

The second mechanism of assimilation was the French language. It was used after the revolution as a means of homogenisation and a tool for republican propaganda. For the Jacobins, speech had to be "one like the republic" [20] (p.72). The patois, a pejorative term used to describe non-Parisian French and regional languages[1] was repressed [21]. Emmanuel Le Roy Ladurie [22] explained it as a barter relationship, where the "linguistic periphery," (p. 492) would give up its languages in exchange for the gift of the French identity, which would provide benefits such as political participation, enlightenment and education. While, the linguistic periphery is almost extinct today except for some islands of resistance in Brittany, the Basque country and Corsica [23], the mechanism is still enforced in other ways. Government action in contemporary times has revolved around the defence of French against the "invasion" of English. In 1992, French was entrenched in the constitution as the language of the republic. The same year, in a revealing twist, the State Council, the highest administrative court and the Constitutional Council, the highest constitutional court in the country annulled its ratification of the European Charter for Regional or Minority languages after discovering that it would lead to the use of regional languages in the public service. In 1994, the Toubon Law made the use of French mandatory in the computing and marketing sectors where English was seen as unduly gaining influence.

The third mechanism military service, was instituted in 1798 and stems from the Jourdan Law. Alongside public schools, military service is credited for helping to turn peasants into Frenchmen [24]. By recruiting millions of people who would have to leave their places of residence, the army became a meeting place for people of different cultural and socioeconomic backgrounds, where they were able to develop a common sense of belonging [25, 26]. Rogers Brubaker asserts that "[they] reinforced each other: The school inculcated military virtues; the army taught language, literacy, and citizenship" [27] (p. 108). Citizenship was a political status of individuals as well as a particular quality of a political system whereby individuals held equal rights [28]. In 1889, military service was extended to foreign residents for assimilationist purposes. It was feared that foreign residents could cluster into enclaves and develop negative feelings towards France. In 1996, the issue of conscription became controversial as President Jacques Chirac moved to

[1] Such as Auvergnat, Occitan, Provençal etc.

suspend it as part of a large restructuring of the army. Opponents of the decision argued that the army had functioned as a melting pot and had instilled civic education as well as other skills, while those agreeing with Chirac's intentions insisted that this function could be accomplished by other institutions [29].

The fourth mechanism was centralised government. At its inception, it was based on the 'département' (department); an administrative unit which was created in the aftermath of the French Revolution as the foundation of a new system of centralisation. Unlike the pre-revolutionary centralised system which was put under the responsibility of the King [30], the 'département' was conceived to promote equality between the regions of France. In particular, 'the two Frances' the richer north and the poorer south, divided along the Saint-Malo-Geneva line [31], between Parisians and the Provinces (the rest of the country) who were then considered so backward that they were called a country of savages [32, 33, 34].

The fifth mechanism, citizenship, was embodied by individual patriotism. France was one of the main countries of jus soli - citizenship based on birth in the territory - which it rolled out to the third and second generation of immigrants respectively in 1851 and 1889. Attempts by Former President Jacques Chirac to roll it back in 1986 were defeated because of its (nationally) sacrosanct character. As a result of this, France has more generous naturalisation policies[2] than, for example, Germany which has traditionally relied on jus sanguinis - citizenship acquisition by blood or descent [35].

Yet, in order to avoid a creation of solidarity in communities that would be considered a threat to the melting pot, citizenship was conceived as an individual not a group ascription [36]. As Rémy Leveau and Dominique Schnapper [37] recount, the Comte de Clermont Tonnère, one of the architects of the French constitution during the revolution, declared that: "one must refuse everything to Jews as a nation and grant everything to Jews as individuals… They must be citizens as individuals" (pp. 29-30). France has always refused to keep any statistics on ethnicity, race or religion, a fact that has hampered research on French immigration [38]. Due to the notion of ethnicity being weak in jus soli and accusations made by André Siegfried in 1946 against the unassimilability of (some) non-Western immigrants,[3] the idea of intentionality became popular. This became a form of patriotism and was referred to by Ernest Renan [39] as a 'daily plebiscite' that amongst other

[2] France was the first country in Western Europe to naturalise Jews in 1791 in the aftermath of its revolution.

[3] Particularly the Beurs, the second and third generation Muslim immigrants from North Africa

things, required immigrants to pay allegiance to their new country rather than their country of origin.

With centralisation and military service progressively losing salience as various economic reforms were introduced, education, the French language and Republican citizenship remained the key mechanisms of reproduction of the national culture. However, rising concerns about 'the degree of openness' of this model, 'the mechanism of *becoming* French' and assimilation in general, ushered in new debates about individual autonomy or freedom of choice. This 'new idea of assimilation' with more relaxed citizenship rules that became widespread in western Europe, was called with some inaccuracy "integration" [40] (p. 5) and came into being with a new philosophical currency, "liberal nationalism" [41]. (p. 239)

## David Miller's Liberal Nationalism

Like Republicanism, liberal nationalism gives preference to the idea of a national culture. Nations have a right to self-determination, that is, to preserve their national identity [42]. David Miller [43] defines a "nation" as "a community (1) constituted by shared belief and mutual commitment, (2) extended in history, (3) active in character, (4) connected to a particular territory, and (5) marked off from other communities by its distinct public culture" (p. 27). Thus culture and nationality are the mechanisms for forging trust and solidarity. These two elements are essential for the maintenance of the welfare state as well as an active citizenship associated with Republicanism.

Veering away from French Republicanism, Miller does not condone coercing immigrants to adopt the dominant culture but rather seeks to encourage them to do so. This is because of his concerns for individual autonomy, where immigrants are asked to 'privatise' themselves, that is, to keep their cultural beliefs and practices to the private sphere as long as they do not hurt others. Privatised individuals are not expected to give up their cultural identity but they are expected to renounce those practices that are deemed 'illiberal', such as forced marriages and female genital mutilation (FGM).[4] They are not, however, asked to renounce those cultural beliefs that can also be considered 'illiberal' such as the belief in the superiority of men over women. Miller, for example, would not support the ban of the burqa that

[4] Which are practised in some countries in Africa and the Middle East.

French authorities have recently instituted [44] because he believes that immigrants only need to accept the liberal minimum by tolerating the existence of opposing arguments [45].

Moreover, Miller recognises that a national culture is open to various interpretations because it is no longer completely homogenous but is a confluence of different lifestyles from vegetarians to Goths to Rastafarians [46]. Here, the relationship is not unilateral as in the republican model where minorities are expected to adopt the dominant culture but is instead bi-lateral or multilateral. An exchange takes places between the national culture and the immigrants' culture which modifies both. However, this exchange does tend to remain unequal and more favourable to the dominant culture. In this model, foreigners' cultural elements are only allowed if they seem to be acceptable to the resident majority[5] [47].

In summary, the idea emerging here is one of two spheres: a public sphere which is the place of politics, economics and law [48] where, it is claimed to be neutral towards different conceptions of the good and a private sphere which is the realm of religion and minorities' cultures. It is within this private sphere that immigrants are allowed to do whatever they want, provided that no harm is caused to the public. Likewise, Miller promotes a republican form of citizenship where the citizen is active and involved in the daily life of the community (Renan's 'daily plebiscite') in contrast to the liberal rights model where they are only united by a set of rights. An active citizen is, "someone who plays an active role in shaping the future direction of his or her society through political debate and decision-making" [49] (p. 53). This view entails reciprocal obligations and a tacit quasi-contract between immigrants and the state [50]. The state must not only guarantee equal citizenship and neutrality in the form of non-discrimination but it should also provide equal opportunities to immigrants. This entails equal access to public goods and any extra measures to address socioeconomic inequalities [51] provided they do not impose excessive costs or jeopardise the existing legal and cultural frameworks.

An example of the clash between these two spheres of influence is the case of Mandla vs. Dowell Lee in 1983. Mandla, a turban-wearing Sikh pupil was denied access to a private English school because his turban and long hair violated the school's uniform code. For Miller [52], the Sikh community would have been held responsible for this clash. This is because Miller

[5] For example, Indian curry, Chinese foods, African Djembe (drumming), Latin-American salsa dance and yoga practice and philosophy are part of Britain's cultural repertoire today

considers wearing a turban a cultural practice that can be dropped, at will.[6] For him, it is a choice and not an ascriptive feature like a physical disability, race or gender [53]. Miller's perspective on citizenship allows for programmes of redistribution targeting immigrants, but it would not allow religious courts like the Beth Din or the Islamic Sharia Council in Britain, which adjudicates civil disputes respectively between consenting Jewish and Muslim parties. Miller's views also do not entail the existence of a separate educational system as in England, where religious groups own schools and formulate their own curriculum but still receive funding from the government (Qualifications and Curriculum Authority 2004)[7] [54]. In return, immigrants are requested to be active citizens. For Miller, that means being law-abiding, voting and—as with Republicanism—engaging in all kinds of civic activities: protests, social activities, being members of conservation groups and supplying information to the police if needed. However, he does not expect immigrants to adopt all the ways of long-established groups particularly in trivial issues. For example, Pakistanis or West Indians (Afro Caribbeans) who have immigrated to the UK need not support the English cricket team to be true patriots [55] as dictated by the "Tebbit test." Norman Tebbit, a Conservative British politician, said in 1990 that the real test of nationality for an immigrant from India or Jamaica was to support the English cricket team when it plays India or the West Indies [56]. Miller asserts that immigrants should strive to find work and be self-supporting as the perception of immigrants' over-reliance on state welfare is a major source of anti-immigrant sentiment. Miller also advocates that immigrants should take up arms in the event of war, even if the aggressor is their country of origin, because citizenship is a contract of mutual protection [57]. Miller believes that naturalised home-grown terrorists should be deprived of their citizenship. He also believes that candidates for naturalisation should also be required to pass civic and language fluency tests in order to obtain citizenship. The same goes for compulsory civic integration contracts in which

[6] The House of Lords (The highest Law Courts in the UK) upheld the appeal by the then Commission for Racial Equality (CRE) against the original decision of legal exclusion (discrimination). They found in favour of CRE and pronounced that the school exclusion was in direct contravention of the 1976 Race Relations Act, and was a discriminatory act, as Sikhs were considered to be an ethnic group in their own right.

[7] These schools are inspected by OFSTED (the UK's School inspectorate), as they are still required to meet the minimum standards of the National Curriculum, especially for the core academic subjects; Maths, English and Science. However, it is also worth noting that in the UK there has been a long tradition of the existence of Faith schools for both Anglican and Catholic Christians that have been and continue to be 'maintained' under state control (funding). Religious education "is a component of the basic curriculum, to be taught alongside the National Curriculum in all maintained schools." (p. 17)

some immigrants are requested to undertake language and professional training as a prerequisite for state financial support [58].

## THEORIES OF MULTICULTURALISM

Multicultural theory emerged as a critique of assimilationist policies and thinking with regard to the formation of ethnic enclaves and continued socioeconomic disparities between natives, immigrants and their descendants. Horace M. Kallen [59] is said to have crafted the concept of 'cultural pluralism' in his lectures between 1905 – 1907 before formally introducing the idea in his 1924 book *Cultural Pluralism and the American Idea An Essay in Social Philosophy.* One of the first books on the subject was also Nathan Glazer's *Affirmative Discrimination: Ethnic Inequality and Public Policy* [60] but its important precursor was Inis Claude's *National Minorities: An International Problem* [61]. The first multiculturalist policies in the West were instituted by the Canadian, Australian, and American governments in the 1970s. Multicultural theory criticises assimilation on three main grounds. The first critique is that the separation of the public and private spheres is superficial. In reality, it is a continuum [62, 63]. Religion, cultural practices and beliefs, which include the moral education given at home, tend to intrude into the public sphere as seen in the case of Mandla vs. Dowell Lee and as mentioned previously in the 1989 "foulard affair" [64, 65]. The state also interferes in the private sphere by extending its prerogatives to matters which relate to family and community well-being through social welfare provisions like family counselling and the education system.

The second critique is that the public sphere and its alleged civic and public culture are not neutral but are hegemonic. Public culture tends to be regarded as the majoritarian culture and even nationalism [66]. Any public culture by default then bears the hallmarks of a religion and a language that are associated with the history and experiences of the majority group [67]. France, for example, follows the Gregorian Christian calendar and observes Christian holidays. Its language is that of the Gallic majority. Defenders of multiculturalism argue that pressure is exercised on minorities to modify [68, 69], their cultures as these are seen as inferior [70]. This hegemony reflects the power of a class of majority decision makers, mostly white males, whose (implicit) cultural biases impact on standards and evaluations used in institutional areas such as education and employment [71]. Minorities, despite their intense efforts to join the mainstream, can find that they are never totally accepted because they are often seen as the “Other” [72].

The third critique, which flows from the previous one, is that universal equal rights and the notion of equal treatment embodied in anti-discrimination legislation do not easily translate into reality. Tools of evaluation and recruitment in society such as standardised tests, foreign degree equivalences and the merit system are skewed against ethnic minorities and women, due to cultural and racial biases against their foreign non-Western qualifications, skin colour, gender, customs, accents, language skills, and cultural differences [73].

To illustrate these points, Bhikhu Parekh [74] interprets the case of Mandla vs. Dowell Lee in a different light to David Miller. He writes that:

> …opportunity is a subject-dependent concept... and not an opportunity for an individual if she lacks the capacity, the cultural disposition or the necessary cultural knowledge to take advantage of it. A Sikh is in principle free to send his son to a school that bans turbans, but for all practical purposes it is closed to him.
> (p. 241)

Prominent multiculturalists such as Charles Taylor, Iris Marion Young and Bhikhu Parekh advocate the recognition of cultures and various forms of group rights. I will now briefly outline their main arguments.

## Charles Taylor and the ‘Politics of Recognition’

Following Frantz Fanon [75], Immanuel Wallerstein [76], and Gunnar Myrdal [77], Charles Taylor [78] asserts that the non-recognition or misrecognition of minorities’ identities is a source of harm; manifesting itself in moral distress and low self-esteem. He goes on to propose that every culture has a meaning for its practitioners. Taylor’s central thesis is that our identity is partly shaped by recognition or its absence, often by the misrecognition of others, and so a person or group of people can suffer real damage and real distortion, if the society around them mirrors back a confining, demeaning or contemptible picture of themselves. Non-recognition or misrecognition can inflict harm and can be a form of oppression that imprisons people in false, distorted and reduced modes of being [79]. Like Georg Wilhelm Friedrich Hegel [80] and before him, Johann Gottfried Herder [81], Taylor suggests that one of the most important aspects of human life is its “dialogical nature” [82] (p. 32), a phenomenon which, he says, cuts across two spheres. Firstly, in the intimate sphere, where we understand the formation of identity and the self as taking place in a continuing dialogue and struggle with significant others. Secondly, in the public sphere, where a politics of equal recognition comes to play an increasingly important role.

For Taylor, being 'oneself' is constructed upon this interaction with the community. He believes that true happiness lies in being "oneself," being "authentic" [83] (pp. 29-30) and not trying to be someone else.[8] Taylor believes that the state must recognise minority cultures and not denigrate them if that is what they conceive as the 'good life'. He also proposes that the state is responsible for providing each individual the opportunity to pursue happiness. For Taylor, simple equal rights that entail procedural equality do not go far enough to recognise what is "specific" to everyone and the "ways" in which citizens differ [84]. (pp. 39-41) In other words, assimilation does not cede enough respect to personal autonomy; the right of people to determine their identity, individually or collectively.

Taylor asserts that procedural liberalism can quickly prove inadequate in a context marked by increased diversity and the desire of communities to keep their culture. Taylor laments the tyranny of a one-sided individualism that is at the heart of the idea that autonomy exists when we detach ourselves from others. The mechanisms of implementation for this policy are, as for the French melting pot, public education and language. But contrary to melting pot assimilationist models, where one language and one set of values are emphasised, a multicultural curriculum teaches minority cultures and languages to majority children and vice-versa. Thus, if a society like Quebec considers the preservation of French a common and precious good, as illustrated by Quebec's Bill 101, it is legitimate that it should be allowed to do so, provided that it also shows respect for diversity and human rights.

Adopted in 1977, the Charter of the French Language, Bill 101 [85] (p. 35) sought:

> to make French the only official language of Quebec; to make French the compulsory language of education in Quebec, except for the indigenous anglophone minority; to make French the language of public administration in Quebec; to make French the language of work in the private sector in Quebec; to make French the language of commerce and publicity

[8] Like the slangs "wannabe" or "whitize"imply that are directed towards African-Americans and Africans in France, respectively, who are said by their peers to be trying to emulate white manners and mannerisms.

Although it eventually failed, the Meech Lake Agreement signed in 1987 re-affirmed Quebec as a distinct society within Canada at the same time that it recognised the rights of anglophone Quebeckers within the Province.

Another example is New Zealand's official biculturalism inherited from the 1840 Treaty of Waitangi. This agreement delineates relationships between Māori (natives) and Pākehā (European settlers). It formally puts both cultures on the same level but also confers special status to the Māori community as the spiritual and cultural custodians of the land. This special status has allowed them to claim collective rights of a socioeconomic nature such as rights to the seabed and foreshore. The Treaty of Waitangi Act, established in 1975, is administered by a tribunal which has, "exclusive authority to determine the meaning and effect of the Treaty as it is embodied in the two texts [Māori and English] and to decide issues raised by the difference between them" [86] (Section 5 (2)). Schedule 2 of the Treaty also establishes the Waitangi Tribunal as a Commission of Inquiry under the Commissions of Inquiry Act 1908 to convene over land rights issues. Whilst Taylor limits group rights to historic (indigenous) minorities, Iris Marion Young envisages even larger categories such as women, religious denominations and lesbian, gays, bisexual and transgender groups (LGBT).

## Iris Marion Young and the 'Politics of Difference'

Iris Marion Young [87] supports a 'politics of difference' as a means of fighting social injustice. For Young, the recognition of cultural differences empowers and liberates people from various forms of social oppression: including racism and sexism. She writes (p. 259), "[t]he concept of the social group has become politically important because recent emancipatory and leftist social movements have mobilized around group identity rather than exclusively class or economic interests….[S]uch mobilization has consisted in embracing…. devalued racial or ethnic identity" as well as "[t]he women's movement…"

Valorising minorities and their cultures helps to relativise the dominant culture but also challenges its claim that it is neutral and universal. This compels members of the dominant culture to regard their culture as just one of among many. Finally, the 'politics of difference' encourages group solidarity, as opposed to liberal individualism which serves just to liberate any one particular group. It is to this end that Young advocates three ways of successfully implementing a strategy for a 'politics of difference'.

The first way, directly addresses cultural issues that are as Taylor argues, centred on multicultural and multilingual education. Young believes that governments must provide minorities, who represent a significant percentage of the population like Spanish-speaking Americans, African-Americans and Native Americans, the opportunities to retain their language and culture. In practical terms, this means providing education and public information in their languages or dialects.

The second mechanism is what Young refers to as comparative worth policies. By this she means the reversal of cultural biases in the measurement of the worth of female-dominated occupations. This could be done, for example, through the creation of schemes that guarantee similar wage structures for female-dominated jobs like nursing that equate to male-dominated jobs in industries involving similar degrees of skill, difficulty, stress, and so on. In other words, to be meaningful, these schemes, she suggests, will have to be gender-conscious and will have to disregard gender-neutral criteria against which women are often at a disadvantage.

The third way is affirmative action. Young declares that affirmative action is not only meant to redress past inequalities but also to compensate, "for the cultural biases of standards and evaluators used by the school or employers" [88]. (p. 271) Young is not concerned with equal treatment but with equal outcome. She agrees that affirmative action programmes violate equal treatment because one needs race or gender-conscious criteria for the promotion of disadvantaged groups. However, for Young, the main 'problem' is not the social conditions of minorities but the (implicit) biases of the tools of evaluation and merit. For her, these biases already do not represent equal treatment so only a strong policy of affirmative action can ensure a better numerical representation of minorities (and their issues).

In that respect, Young supports a form of group rights which she calls "differentiated citizenship" [89], (p. 251) that is, the group representation of minorities (people of colour, women, and homosexuals) in the decision-making process. She argues that this will give these minorities a voice in setting the agenda and guarantee both procedural and substantive fairness. When everyone is represented, everyone's needs are more likely to be met. Group representation also gives to minorities a sense of entitlement and produces a richer body of knowledge about social issues.

Young does not prescribe any particular mode of representation as she feels that this "depends on the political situation, on the nature of the structural cleavages of the polity, possible trade-offs...and the institutional context for representation" [90]. (p. 149) As an example, the system of representation set for the Māori in New Zealand was besieged by all sorts of problems regarding the voting system and the design of electoral districts, until a proportional electoral system allowed a Māori party to emerge. Nevertheless, she supports greater diversity of representation in the policy making process.

## Bhikhu Parekh's 'Pluralist Universalism'

Like Taylor and Young, Bhikhu Parekh asserts that recognition is an essential component of people's identity and its absence can cause harm [91]. He defines multiculturalism as "a body of beliefs and practices in terms of which a group of people understand themselves and the world and organize their individual and collective lives" [92]. (pp. 2-3) Furthermore, he argues that individuals are all culturally embedded. For him, no culture can be termed worthless. However for Parekh, this does not mean that cultures all have the same value just that "*all cultures have worth and deserve basic respect*" as he says, that "they are not equally worthy and do not merit equal respect" [93]. (p. 177)[9] Although a Muslim girl, for example, might be unwilling to swim in shorts, or undergo an internal examination by a male doctor; or a Sikh boy not want to go to school without his turban, Parekh [94] would advocate in both instances that the wider society should accommodate such demands.[10]

Lastly, Parekh [95] argues that cultural diversity as a source of enrichment is desirable and unavoidable, while every culture itself is plural. Although he is against some cultural practices including polygamy and FGM, he explains that, immigrants' practices such as arranged marriages and the wearing of the Islamic veil [96] that produce no harm to others but are viewed by the majority as illiberal, represent different notions of the good life. In this vein, Parekh argues that, it is only through an intercommunal dialogue or a "pluralist universalism" [97] (p. 126) that a consensus can be negotiated for everyone's benefit [98]. Parekh also supports the introduction of multicultural education in all schools not only those where a sizeable part of the population has a non-Western background as suggested by David Miller. His argument is that a monocultural education is Eurocentric and is more likely to breed intolerance

---

[9] Of course, this is an ambivalent statement at best, as it begs the question, as to who decides on levels of worthiness and respect. This also potentially puts him at odds with Young's 'politics of difference' where all marginalised groups are equally encouraged to strive for equality and recognition.

[10] Except when they are patently unreasonable or excessively costly (perhaps qualifying the second half of his statement), or else it would makes it difficult for these people to integrate according to Parekh.

and racism. Parekh believes that exposing students to other cultures and histories that are positive, opens their imaginations and increases their respect and understanding of other cultures. So, if a school includes colonialism in its history curriculum, it should include both Joseph Conrad's Western classic *Heart of Darkness* [99] and Chinua Achebe's *Things Fall Apart* [100]. Achebe's book has consistently been ranked among the best literary works of the 20th century (or indeed of all time) [101, 102]. Parekh would regard this as showing that non-Western works can also be canonical [103]. Achebe offers an important perspective on the encounter between the West and Africa which is both instructive and different to Conrad's view [104, 105].

Parekh argues that misrecognition also has a material basis if which left unresolved, can pose a serious threat to the stability of society [106]. He predicts that the dominant group will (inevitably) refuse to acquiesce to the "rigorous critique of the dominant culture" and the radical "restructuring [of] the prevailing inequalities of economic and political power" [107]. (p. 343) Demands for a 'politics of recognition', Parekh warns, may also result in political contestation and even violence, such as the 2005 French riots involving youths of Arab and black African descent [108]. Like Young, Parekh [109] argues for the group representation of minorities in public policy making and the public sphere. But, for him, what matters, is not the form that these rights take but their content and even more importantly, their implementation. Despite its importance, equal citizenship is not enough. Parekh maintains that minorities must also secure a sense of belonging, which derives from a sense of being accepted and not merely tolerated. This means perhaps redefining the concept of national identity in terms that are more inclusive and non-ethnic.[11] He argues [110] (p. 84):

> Assimilationism is not as simple and smooth a process as the assimilationist imagines. The assimilating person is never quite sure when she has become assimilated fully and whether she is accepted. She is therefore anxious to prove to herself and others that she has assimilated, is generally loud and earnest to show that she is not a counterfeit, which makes her strangeness even more visible and comical. She is also constantly at the mercy of others, who alone are in a position to certify whether or not, and how much, she has assimilated, and remains permanently subordinate and heteronomous. As if this is not enough, she needs to keep pressuring other members of her group to assimilate, because if they do not that reflects badly on her and is embarrassing. Since some of them might not, she must join others in condemning them

[11] Which is a little conundrum considering the non-ethnic premise of assimilation.

or at least disown and keep her distance from them, with all the moral and psychological corruption this involves.

## CONCLUSION

As suggested at the beginning of this chapter, scholars have conceived very different frameworks around multiculturalism and assimilation. However, a closer look shows that what assimilationist and possibly liberal nationalist views have in common, at their heart, is the disapproval of minority cultures and the subsequent prominence given to their majority cultures, where the state, in liberal nationalism, is supposed to avoid any interference and uses persuasion rather than coercion. Multiculturalist perspectives, on the other hand tend to link immigrants' wellbeing to the existence of a thriving culture of their own. Cultural diversity is seen as enriching for the country's own culture and that the state has the duty of promoting this diversity. However, both multiculturalism and assimilation (and liberal nationalism) do appear to converge on the concept of a *liberal minimum*, where certain practices or beliefs such as polygamy or FGM are viewed as unacceptable by the resident majority and are not tolerated in any sphere of influence. It is this idea of the liberal minimum that seems to unite the sometimes conflicting views of David Miller's liberal nationalism, Charles Taylor's 'politics of recognition', Iris Marion Young's 'politics of difference' and Bhikhu Parekh's 'pluralist universalism'.[12]

## REFERENCES

[1] Hollifield, J. F. (2000). The Politics of International Migration: How Can We Bring the State Back in? In C. B. Brettell, and J. F. Hollifield (Eds.), *Migration Theory: Talking Across Disciplines* (pp. 162-172). New York, London: Routledge.

[2] Hartmann, D., and Gerteis, J. (2005). Dealing with Diversity: Mapping Multiculturalism in Sociological Terms. *Sociological Theory, 23*(2), 218-240.

[3] Brubaker, R. (1992). *Citizenship and Nationhood in France and Germany.* Cambridge, MA: Harvard University Press.

[12] As mentioned earlier, the concept of a liberal minimum throws up interesting questions about who decides what the minimum is and how this is managed.

[4] Miller, D. (1995). *On Nationality.* New York: Oxford University Press.
[5] Kymlicka, W., and Norman, W. (Eds.). (2000). *Citizenship in Diverse Societies.* Oxford: Oxford University Press.
[6] Armitage, A. (1995). *Comparing the Policy of Aboriginal Assimilation. Australia, Canada and New Zealand.* Vancouver: University of British Columbia Press.
[7] Roberts, S. H. (1929). *History of French Colonial Policy (1870- 1925).* London: P.S. King and Son Ltd.
[8] Noiriel, G. (1999). Immigration and National Memory in Current French Historiography. *IMIS-Beiträge, Heft 10*, 39-56.
[9] Noiriel, G. (1999). Immigration and National Memory in Current French Historiography. *IMIS-Beiträge, Heft 10*, 39-56.
[10] Michelet, J. (1875). *Tableau de la France: géographie physique, politique et morale.* Paris: Lacroix.
[11] Noiriel, G. (1999). Immigration and National Memory in Current French Historiography. *IMIS-Beiträge, Heft 10*, 39-56.
[12] Guiomar, J.-Y. (1997). Vidal's Geography of France. In P. Nora (Ed.), *Realms of Memory. The Construction of the French Past, II, Traditions* (A. Goldhammer, Trans., pp. 187-209). New York: Columbia University Press.
[13] Vidal de la Blache, P. (1941). *Tableau de la Géographie de France.* Manchester and London: Manchester University Press, London Hachette.
[14] Brubaker, R. (1992). *Citizenship and Nationhood in France and Germany.* Cambridge, MA: Harvard University Press.
[15] Schnapper, D. (1991). *La France de l'intégration.* Paris: Gallimard.
[16] Brubaker, R. (1992). *Citizenship and Nationhood in France and Germany.* Cambridge, MA: Harvard University Press.
[17] Vie Publique. (2006, May 30). *L'intégration républicaine fonctionne-t-elle encore face à la diversité culturelle?* Retrieved August 31, 2015, from Vie Publique: http://www.vie-publique.fr/decouverte-institutions/citoyen/enjeux/crise-citoyennete/integration-republicaine-fonctionne-t-elle-encore-face-diversite-culturelle.html
[18] Kritzman, L. D. (1997). Foreward. In P. Nora (Ed.), *Realms of Memory. The Construction of the French Past, I, Conflicts and Divisions* (pp. ix-xiv). New York: Columbia University Press.
[19] Benhabib, S. (2004). *The Right of Others. Aliens, Residents and Citizens.* Cambridge, UK: Cambridge University Press.

[20] Weber, E. (1976). *Peasants into Frenchmen: The Modernization of Rural France, 1870 - 1914.* Stanford: Standford University Press.

[21] Le Roy Ladurie, E. (1997). *L'historien, le chiffre et le texte.* Paris: Fayard.

[22] Le Roy Ladurie, E. (1997). *L'historien, le chiffre et le texte.* Paris: Fayard.

[23] Vie Publique. (2006, May 30). *L'intégration républicaine fonctionne-t-elle encore face à la diversité culturelle?* Retrieved August 31, 2015, from Vie Publique: http://www.vie-publique.fr/decouverte-institutions/citoyen/enjeux/crise-citoyennete/integration-republicaine-fonctionne-t-elle-encore-face-diversite-culturelle.html

[24] Weber, E. (1976). *Peasants into Frenchmen: The Modernization of Rural France, 1870 - 1914.* Stanford: Standford University Press.

[25] Braudel, F. (1986). *L'identité de la France. Espace et Histoire.* Paris: Arthaud Flammarion.

[26] La Documentation Française. (2015, August 31). *Le débat sur le service civil obligatoire.* Retrieved August 31, 2015, from La Documentation Française: http://www.ladocumentationfrancaise.fr/dossiers/d000079-service-civil-volontaire-ou-service-civil-obligatoire/le-debat-sur-le-service-civil-obligatoire

[27] Brubaker, R. (1992). *Citizenship and Nationhood in France and Germany.* Cambridge, MA: Harvard University Press.

[28] Bauböck, R. (1991). Migration and Citizenship. *New Community, 18*(1), 27-48.

[29] Fitchett, J. (1996, February 22). *Chirac to Unveil Plans for an All-Volunteer French Army.* Retrieved August 31, 2015, from The New York Times: http://www.nytimes.com/1996/02/22/news/22iht-army.t_0.html

[30] Noiriel, G. (1996). *The French Melting Pot: Immigration, Citizenship and National Identity.* Minneapolis: University of Minnesota Press.

[31] Chartier, R. (1996). The Saint-Malo-Geneva Line. In *Realms of Memory. The Construction of the French Past, I, Conflicts and Divisions* (pp. 467-496). New York: Columbia University Press.

[32] Weber, E. (1976). *Peasants into Frenchmen: The Modernization of Rural France, 1870 - 1914.* Stanford: Standford University Press.

[33] Corbin, A. (1996). Divisions of Time and Space. In P. Nora (Ed.), *Realms of Memory. The Construction of the French Past, I, Conflicts and Divisions* (pp. 427-464). New York: Columbia University Press.

[34] Alexander, J. C. (2001). Theorizing the 'Modes of Incorporation': Assimilation, Hyphenation and Multiculturalism as Varieties of Civil Participation. *Sociological Theory*, 237-249.

[35] Brubaker, R. (1992). *Citizenship and Nationhood in France and Germany.* Cambridge, MA: Harvard University Press

[36] Noiriel, G. (1996). *The French Melting Pot: Immigration, Citizenship and National Identity.* Minneapolis: University of Minnesota Press.

[37] Leveau, R., and Schnapper, D. (1987). Religion et politique. juifs et musulmans maghrébins en France. *Revue française de science politique, 37*(6), 855-890.

[38] Bleich, E. (2003). *Race Politics in Britain and France. Ideas and Policy making since the 1960s.* Cambridge: Cambridge University Press.

[39] Renan, E. (1996[1882]). What is Nation? In G. Eley, and R. G. Suny (Eds.), *Becoming National: A Reader* (pp. 41-55). New York and Oxford: Oxford University Press.

[40] Joppke, C., and Morawska, E. (Eds.). (2003). *Toward Assimilationism and Citizenship. Immigrants in Liberal nation-states.* Basingstoke: Palgrave Macmillan.

[41] Joppke, C. (2004). The Retreat of Multiculturalism in the Liberal State: Theory and Policy. *British Journal of Sociology, 55*(2), 237-257.

[42] Tamir, Y. (1993). *Liberal Nationalism.* Princeton, NJ: Princeton University Press.

[43] Miller, D. (1995). *On Nationality.* New York: Oxford University Press.

[44] BBC News. (2010, July 13). *French MPs vote to ban Islamic full veil in public.* Retrieved August 31, 2015, from BBC News: http://www.bbc.co.uk/news/10611398

[45] Miller, D. (2008). Immigrants, Nations, and Citizenship. *Journal of Political Philosophy, 16*(4), 371–390.

[46] Miller, D. (2000). *Citizenship and National Identity.* Cambridge: Polity Press.

[47] Hansen, R. (2000). *Citizenship and Immigration in Post-War Britain.* Oxford: Oxford University Press.

[48] Rex, J. (1996). *Ethnic minorities in the modern nation state: Working papers in the theory of multiculturalism and political integration.* Houndmills, Basingstoke, Hampshire, London, New York: MacMillan Press.

[49] Miller, D. (2000). *Citizenship and National Identity.* Cambridge: Polity Press.

[50] Miller, D. (2008). Immigrants, Nations, and Citizenship. *Journal of Political Philosophy, 16*(4), 371–390.

[51] Miller, D. (2008). Immigrants, Nations, and Citizenship. *Journal of Political Philosophy, 16*(4), 371–390.

[52] Miller, D. (2000). *Citizenship and National Identity.* Cambridge: Polity Press.

[53] Mendus, S. (2002). Choice, Chance and Multiculturalism. In P. Kelly (Ed.), *Multiculturalism Reconsidered* (pp. 31-44). Cambridge: Polity Press.

[54] Qualifications and Curriculum Authority. (2004, October). *The National Curriculum: Handbook for secondary teachers in England www.nc.uk.net.* Retrieved August 31, 2015, from http://webarchive.nationalarchives.gov.uk/: http://webarchive.nationalarchives.gov.uk/20130401151715/http://www.education.gov.uk/publications/eOrderingDownload/QCA-04-1374.pdf

[55] Miller, D. (2008). Immigrants, Nations, and Citizenship. *Journal of Political Philosophy, 16*(4), 371–390.

[56] Miller, D. (2008). Immigrants, Nations, and Citizenship. *Journal of Political Philosophy, 16*(4), 371–390.

[57] Miller, D. (2008). Immigrants, Nations, and Citizenship. *Journal of Political Philosophy, 16*(4), 371–390.

[58] Entzinger, H. (2003). The Rise and Fall of Multiculturalism. In C. Joppke, and E. Morawska (Eds.), *Towards assimilation and citizenship: Immigrants in liberal nationstates* (pp. 59-86). Basingstoke: Palgrave Macmillan.

[59] Kallen, H. M. (1956[1924]). *Cultural Pluralism and the American Idea An Essay in Social Philosophy.* Philadelphia: University of Pennsylvania Press.

[60] Glazer, N. (1975). *Affirmative Discrimination: Ethnic Inequality and Public Policy.* Cambridge, MA: Harvard University Press.

[61] Claude, I. L. (1955). *National Minorities: An International Problem.* Cambridge, MA: Harvard University Press.

[62] Parekh, B. (2000). *Rethinking Multiculturalism: Cultural Diversity and Political Theory.* Cambridge, MA: Harvard University Press.

[63] Taylor, C. (1994). The Politics of Recognition. In A. Gutmann (Ed.), *Multiculturalism: Examining the Politics of Recognition* (pp. 25-74). Princeton, NJ: Princeton University Press.

[64] Benhabib, S. (2004). *The Right of Others. Aliens, Residents and Citizens.* Cambridge, UK: Cambridge University Press.

[65] Bouteldja, N. (2005, February 25). *The reality of l'affaire du foulard.* Retrieved from The Guardian: http://www.theguardian.com/world/2005/feb/25/france.religion

[66] Taylor, C. (1994). The Politics of Recognition. In A. Gutmann (Ed.), *Multiculturalism: Examining the Politics of Recognition* (pp. 25-74). Princeton, NJ: Princeton University Press.

[67] Taylor, C. (1994). The Politics of Recognition. In A. Gutmann (Ed.), *Multiculturalism: Examining the Politics of Recognition* (pp. 25-74). Princeton, NJ: Princeton University Press.

[68] Young, I. M. (1990). *Justice and the Politics of Difference.* Princeton, NJ: Princeton University Press.

[69] Taylor, C. (1994). The Politics of Recognition. In A. Gutmann (Ed.), *Multiculturalism: Examining the Politics of Recognition* (pp. 25-74). Princeton, NJ: Princeton University Press.

[70] Birnbaum, P. (1996). From Multiculturalism to Nationalism. *Political Theory, 24*(1), 33-45.

[71] Young, I. M. (1990). *Justice and the Politics of Difference.* Princeton, NJ: Princeton University Press.

[72] Young, I. M. (1990). *Justice and the Politics of Difference.* Princeton, NJ: Princeton University Press.

[73] Young, I. M. (1989). Polity and Group Difference: A Critique of the Ideal of Universal Citizenship. *Ethics, 99*(2), 250-274.

[74] Parekh, B. (2000). *Rethinking Multiculturalism: Cultural Diversity and Political Theory.* Cambridge, MA: Harvard University Press.

[75] Fanon, F. (1970). *Black Skin, White Masks.* London: Paladin.

[76] Wallerstein, I. (1961). *Africa: The Politics of Independence.* London: Paladin.

[77] Myrdal, G. (1944). *An American Dilemma: The Negro problem and modern democracy.* New York: Harper and Brothers.

[78] Taylor, C. (1994). The Politics of Recognition. In A. Gutmann (Ed.), *Multiculturalism: Examining the Politics of Recognition* (pp. 25-74). Princeton, NJ: Princeton University Press.

[79] Taylor, C. (1994). The Politics of Recognition. In A. Gutmann (Ed.), *Multiculturalism: Examining the Politics of Recognition* (pp. 25-74). Princeton, NJ: Princeton University Press.

[80] Honneth, A. (1995). *The Struggle for Recognition: The Moral Grammar of Social Conflicts.* (J. Anderson, Trans.) Cambridge, MA: Massachusetts Institute of Technology.

[81] Spencer, V. A. (2012). *Herder's Political Thought: A Study of Language, Culture and Community.* Toronto: Toronto University Press.

[82] Taylor, C. (1994). The Politics of Recognition. In A. Gutmann (Ed.), *Multiculturalism: Examining the Politics of Recognition* (pp. 25-74). Princeton, NJ: Princeton University Press.

[83] Taylor, C. (1994). The Politics of Recognition. In A. Gutmann (Ed.), *Multiculturalism: Examining the Politics of Recognition* (pp. 25-74). Princeton, NJ: Princeton University Press.

[84] Taylor, C. (1994). The Politics of Recognition. In A. Gutmann (Ed.), *Multiculturalism: Examining the Politics of Recognition* (pp. 25-74). Princeton, NJ: Princeton University Press.

[85] Hearn, J. (2006). *Rethinking Nationalism: A Critical Introduction.* Basingstoke: Palgrave Macmillan.

[86] Parliamentary Counsel Office. (2014, December 16). *Treaty of Waitangi Act 1975.* Retrieved from New Zealand Legislation: http://www.legislation.govt.nz/act/public/1975/0114/latest/whole.html# DLM435375

[87] Young, I. M. (1989). Polity and Group Difference: A Critique of the Ideal of Universal Citizenship. *Ethics, 99*(2), 250-274.

[88] Young, I. M. (1989). Polity and Group Difference: A Critique of the Ideal of Universal Citizenship. *Ethics, 99*(2), 250-274.

[89] Young, I. M. (1989). Polity and Group Difference: A Critique of the Ideal of Universal Citizenship. *Ethics, 99*(2), 250-274.

[90] Young, I. M. (2000). *Inclusion and Democracy.* Oxford: Oxford University Press.

[91] Parekh, B. (2000). *Rethinking Multiculturalism: Cultural Diversity and Political Theory.* Cambridge, MA: Harvard University Press.

[92] Parekh, B. (2000). *Rethinking Multiculturalism: Cultural Diversity and Political Theory.* Cambridge, MA: Harvard University Press.

[93] Parekh, B. (2000). *Rethinking Multiculturalism: Cultural Diversity and Political Theory.* Cambridge, MA: Harvard University Press.

[94] Parekh, B. (2008). *A New Politics of Identity: Political Principles for an Interdependent World.* Basingstoke: Palgrave Macmillan.

[95] Parekh, B. (2000). *Rethinking Multiculturalism: Cultural Diversity and Political Theory.* Cambridge, MA: Harvard University Press.

[96] Parekh, B. (1996). Minority Practices and Principles of Toleration. *International Migration Review, 30*(1), 251-284.

[97] Parekh, B. (2000). *Rethinking Multiculturalism: Cultural Diversity and Political Theory.* Cambridge, MA: Harvard University Press.

[98] Parekh, B. (1996). Minority Practices and Principles of Toleration. *International Migration Review, 30*(1), 251-284.

[99] Conrad, J. (1990[1902]). *Heart of Darkness.* Mineola, NY: Dover Publications.

[100] Achebe, C. (1958). *Things Fall Apart.* London: Heinemann.

[101] Grossman, L., and Lacayo, R. (2010, January 6). *All-TIME 100 Novels.* Retrieved August 31, 2015, from TIME: http://entertainment.time.com/2005/10/16/all-time-100-novels/slide/all/

[102] The Guardian. (2002, May 8). *The top 100 books of all time.* Retrieved August 31, 2015, from The Guardian: http://www.theguardian.com/world/2002/may/08/books.booksnews

[103] Taylor, C. (1994). The Politics of Recognition. In A. Gutmann (Ed.), *Multiculturalism: Examining the Politics of Recognition* (pp. 25-74). Princeton, NJ: Princeton University Press.

[104] Achebe, C. (2001). An Image of Africa: Conrad's Heart of Darkness. In V. Leitch (Ed.), *The Norton Anthology of Theory and Criticism* (First ed., pp. 1783-1794). New York: Norton and Company.

[105] Watts, C. (1983). 'A Bloody Racist': About Achebe's View of Conrad. *Yearbook of English Studies, 13*(Colonial and Imperial Themes Special), 196-209.

[106] Parekh, B. (2000). *Rethinking Multiculturalism: Cultural Diversity and Political Theory.* Cambridge, MA: Harvard University Press.

[107] Parekh, B. (2000). *Rethinking Multiculturalism: Cultural Diversity and Political Theory.* Cambridge, MA: Harvard University Press.

[108] BBC News Channel. (2005, November 14). *Timeline: French riots.* Retrieved from BBC News: http://news.bbc.co.uk/1/hi/world/europe/4413964.stm

[109] Parekh, B. (2000). *Rethinking Multiculturalism: Cultural Diversity and Political Theory.* Cambridge, MA: Harvard University Press.

[110] Parekh, B. (2008). *A New Politics of Identity: Political Principles for an Interdependent World.* Basingstoke: Palgrave Macmillan.

In: International Perspectives of Multiculturalism ISBN: 978-1-63483-971-6
Editor: Ornette D. Clennon 

*Chapter 2*

# THE ETHICAL IMPLICATIONS OF IDEOLOGICAL AND POLITICAL MULTICULTURALISM IN THE UK

***Ornette D. Clennon****
**Manchester Metropolitan University, Manchester, UK**

## ABSTRACT

In this chapter, Ornette D Clennon examines the relationship between two forms of UK multiculturalism; namely, ideological and political. He also traces how these two inter-related forms of multiculturalism originate from the concept of a national cultural memory. Whilst broadly critiquing David Miller's Liberal Nationalism, which dismisses the notion of a priori belonging in favour of (tacet) civic integration contracts, Clennon builds on Bhikhu Parekh's Pluralist Universalism and Ernest Renan's notion of the "daily plebiscite" to discuss the process of negotiating post-colonial stakeholdership in a national cultural memory.

Clennon argues that stakeholdership within a national cultural memory defines the nature of ideological multiculturalism and its performative political processes of citizenisation. Finally, the chapter explores how multiculturalism, as part of the Human Rights Movement appears to be used by the global 'war on terror' as a political tool of state control.

* Email: o.clennon@mmu.ac.uk.

**Keywords:** multiculturalism, human rights movement, stakeholdership, citizenisation, assimilation, equality and diversity, PREVENT

## INTRODUCTION

Nissa Finney & Ludi Simpson [1] write that in 2001 the terrorist attacks in the US and the urban UK Northwest disturbances (in the same year), "changed the national and international terrain for thinking about integration, segregation, migration and multiculturalism" (p. 3). I would also add the later 2005 London bombings and the 2011 UK national riots to this list. However, despite this change-inducing turbulence, Heidi Mirza [2] (p. 111) observes that, "the more things change, the more they stay the same" concerning the centrality of race and culture for minorities. Mirza implies that when we discuss multiculturalism, there still seems to be a pre-dominant concept of 'Whiteness'[14] that forces other perspectives to be viewed from a point of 'deficit'.

Keeping Mirza's observation in mind, I would like to explore two levels of multiculturalism that can easily be conflated but need to be disaggregated; the ideological and the political.

I would argue that the former is crucial for thinking through issues of identity, belonging and stakeholdership, whilst the latter is equally important for turning these discursive concepts into legislation. In this chapter, I will explore the ethical challenges behind both concepts of multiculturalism.

## ETHICAL IMPLICATIONS OF IDEOLOGICAL MULTICULTURALISM IN THE UK

Looking at Mirza's ideological observations about 'Whiteness' and cultural 'deficit' in the UK, Paul Gilroy [3] (p. 434) explains the occurrence of this dominant discourse as a, "melancholic[15] attachment to its [Britain's]

[14] See Chapter 4 for a fuller discussion about the psychopolitics 'whiteness'.

[15] "Melancholic attachment" is a specific Freudian reference and has been discussed at length by Judith Butler that describes a state of unrequited love, where the "lover" realises he cannot attain love from his "object", so instead of mourning the loss of his "object" (and moving on) he redirects his love of his "object" towards himself. However, he knows that his self-directed love (narcissism) is only a pale substitute for the true "object" of his affections, so he becomes melancholic in this realisation of his loss that he refuses to mourn (or let go of).

vanished pre-eminence" [4]. Here, Gilroy writes that the UK's colonial attachment to its past colours how it views race, culture and history and this form of recollecting has facilitated a revisionist view of British history, which he says has been propounded by popular (TV) historians[16] [5, 6, 7], Pierre Nora [8] would characterise this act of revisionism as post-modernist nation building where our present communication and cultural technologies are able to fashion distinct and self-validating myths from the already existing simulacra of modern memories[17] [9]. I will unpack the importance of the 'post-modern' later when discussing the making of international cultural memories. However, as regards the process of forming a national cultural memory, Gilroy notes that this type of revisionism is a worrying trend in the

---

Even though he cannot attain love from his "object" and has to supply it to himself, he is still attached to the idea of his unattainable "object" and this attachment to this idea of this "object" colours everything he sees around him, sometimes manifesting itself in extreme frustration or even hate. Butler (p. 168) describes this process of self-directed love as the "lover" (ego) "turn[ing] back upon it[him]self" and says that the "lover" is actually defined by this process and would not exist without his melancholic attachment, implying that he needs to manufacture this loss (or create the myth!) in order to define his true identity for himself! This has interesting connotations when this framework is applied to the psyche of a nation.

[16] W.E.B. Du Bois traces a very similar type of historical revisionism that facilitated the construction of a national identity for a post slavery North America, that used racist propaganda about the then 'Negroes' to justify a racial patriarchy, which underpinned the growing democratic identity of the US. Ben Becker, following on from Du Bois, more recently writes about how the African American has been airbrushed from what was called 'Decoration Day', as it is now called 'Memorial Day'. Decoration Day was originally established by former slaves to, "celebrate emancipation and commemorate those who died for that cause." Elsewhere, I extensively discuss the global cultural and political ramifications of this mythologised propaganda and how it shapes contemporary discourse around race and ethnicity.

[17] Tavia Nyong'o brings this aspect of the 'post-modern' vividly to life when he describes how the Internet has transformed our values (or aspirations) of liberal democracy into a panoply of consumer choice. Nyong'o argues that social networking creates a form of 'short circuit' which lulls users into a false sense of both geographical and ideological alliance/complicity. However, this feeling of closeness is only made possible by the product of a neoliberal infrastructure that monetises our supposed alliances. Nyong'o in his specific context of queer activism goes on to say that our (in effect) monetised responses to humanitarian calls for action, before they even have a chance to materialise in the 'real' word, have already added to the capital function of accumulation and dispossession. In other words, our responses that we think reflect our values of liberal democracy are nothing more than 'user-generated content' born out of our privileged position as consumer exercising our consumer choice. Nyong'o characterises this process as "Participation as a Neoliberal Fantasy" (p. 52). This for me brings great insight into how the West's globally exported post-modern cultural memories of liberal democracy are underpinned by its neoliberal infrasturctures that are themselves inherently illiberal, as they (re)produce social inequalities (for more on this, see Chapter 4). Later in this chapter, I explore more fully how cultural memories are institutionalised and marketised as a means of building a national consciousness.

public discourse about race and culture. Gilroy maintains that it tends to erode the, “political significance of racism as an independent issue that requires theoretical consideration beyond economic reduction or the assertion of general theories of ideology” (p. 431). In our present national debate about immigration in the UK, Gilroy’s ‘melancholia’ takes the form of a soft nationalism, where the economically driven process of consolidating national identities[18] is constantly debated without actually addressing its inherent or underlying structures of racial inequality. The rallying cry of this type of soft nationalism tends to be for national or civic unity[19] around ‘British values’ but as Nasar Meer & Tariq Modood [10] observe, “such sentiment ignores…how all forms of prescribed unity, including civic unity, usually retain a majoritarian bias that places the burden of adaptation upon the minority” (p. 188).

What is interesting about this ideological call for civic unity is that it presupposes a single idea of Britishness to which everyone supposedly should ascribe. However, many detractors of political (and ideological) multiculturalism in also viewing it as a single doctrine[20] [11], fail to take into account that there is no overarching political (or ideological) concept of Britishness either. Devolution and the Scottish independence referendum also point to a similar patchwork of policies designed to accommodate a Britishness that is itself an ever-changing ideological and political landscape and one that is set to become even more fluid with the prospect of devolved power given to the English regions. In fact, the recent debate around Scottish Independence pointed towards a demonstrably malleable concept of (Scottish) national identity that was formed by the curating of a national historical narrative. It was precisely this plastic memory of a nation that was used to great political effect to evoke feelings of national pride and self-confidence

[18] i.e., employment markets and national infrastructures in the areas of health and social welfare (political) as well as more mythological national identities (ideological)

[19] Here I will use the term “civic” to imply both the process of local government administration and the sense of “civilian” and their “civil” interactions with civic institutions made possible by their rights as “citizens”. This is a slightly different meaning to “civil rights” where it is understood that these rights are really “human rights” that are administered at state rather than an international level. See Chapter 3 for a full discussion about Civil, Fundamental and Human Rights. I will later discuss the idea of civic unity both culturally in terms of implicit Islamophobic rhetoric aimed at parts of the British Muslim communities and economically in terms of underlying xenophobic sentiment aimed at Eastern European immigrants.

[20] Despite Steven Vertovec & Susan Wessendorf reminding us that it is a, “myriad patchwork of policies, practices and institutional adjustments through which immigrant and ethnic minority accommodation and incorporation are actually undertaken” (p. 6)

(both of which were meant to lead to feelings of readiness for independence). This curated cultural memory almost won the debate. Almost.

## The Role of Cultural Memory

The concept of multiculturalism[21] [12], as both an ideological and political form of civic unity is not only about the fundamental question of how a nation recognises and treats its minorities (political) but also how it manages to assemble a sense of itself by equitably balancing the historical narratives and concerns of both its majorities and minorities (ideological). In the UK, this 'melancholic' call for British values assumes a monistic view of what a nation is by which, "[m]any complicated strands are reduced to a simple tale of essential and enduring national unity" [22] [13]. (para. 2.9, 16) [14] This would very much seem to be an institutional curating of history in order to form a synthetic form of national identity that is very much akin to Jan Assmann & John Czaplicka's concept of a cultural memory that is, "maintained through cultural formation (texts, rites, monuments) and institutional communication (recitation, practice, observance)" (p. 129) [15]. The UK's Referendum on Scottish Independence again showed us that this process of, "select[ing] from all that has gone before that which is distinctive, 'truly ours', and thereby to mark out a unique, shared destiny" [16] (p. 43) cannot be taken so easily for granted. National talks around devolution and independence in the UK have long since invoked a political but also a *cultural* 'multicultural' framework involving our 'sub-state national minorities'[23] [17].

Of Will Kymlicka's three general principles[24] for the political civic integration of minority groups, his third that suggests that nation states should

---

[21] This includes the relatively new concept of interculturalism that supposedly puts a greater emphasis on dialogue and consensus building between cultures. However, Nasar Meer & Tariq Modood note that this is not necessarily a new development in thinking because those concepts of dialogue and communication formed the original idea of multiculturalism, albeit transformed by different national interpretations.

[22] Bridget Byrne observed that the British Citizenship ceremonies that she attended included a form of national storytelling that was designed to relate a simplified version of British history (to which participants were supposed to pledge allegiance), which missed out large parts of Britain's colonial past and its subsequent racism.

[23] Will Kymlicka usefully defines three types of minority groups that are concerned with civic 'integration', namely; indigenous peoples, sub-state nationals and immigrant groups.

[24] Kymlicka's principles are 1. The state belongs to all of its citizens equally 2. All citizens should have equal access to state institutions 3. States should acknowledge historical injustices done to its minorities.

acknowledge the historical injustices done to its minority groups is of greatest interest to me. This acknowledgment pre-supposes an ideological examination and a 'consciousness-raising' of the, "many complicated strands" that comprise the building of a national psyche. This point particularly springs to life from a post-colonial perspective in the UK, with the final mid twentieth century arrival of (economic) migrants from the former colonies of the Caribbean, South East Asia and East Africa. So, in this context of introspection, we have to ask what does this 'melancholic' call for a return to 'British values' actually mean especially in view of a sometimes, brutal British Colonial rule? Precisely into what are (post-colonial) minorities expected to integrate, is an important question. If the basic premise of civic integration involves being legally and civically accepted into an a priori concept of monistic nationhood,[25] we can see that not only does this state of affairs disadvantage minority groups,[26] it actually serves to oppress the very minorities to whom it intends to bring equality by virtue of their erasure from this simplified historical narrative. From a post-colonial perspective, this leaves post-colonial minorities in a strange predicament of having to *ask* to be accorded rights and privileges as citizens in nations they themselves historically helped to build! [18][27]

This 'predicament' of majoritarian amnesia is strongly illustrated by blaming multiculturalism for promoting 'difference' or 'separateness'. The former Shadow Home Secretary, David Davis was reported to have said that Muslims needed to start integrating into mainstream British society, where he proposed a signalled shift away from the policy of multiculturalism that allowed people of different faiths and cultures to settle without expecting them to integrate. Davis went on to write that, "often, the authorities have seemed more concerned with encouraging distinctive identities rather than promoting the common values of nationhood" [19]. This fear of 'difference' was even more recently graphically demonstrated by the Trojan Horse scandal,[28] in

[25] Replete with a simplified and unifying historical narrative

[26] With the application of the 'majoritarian bias' that Nasar Meer & Tariq Modood mention

[27] Bridget Byrne also noticed that in US Citizenship ceremonies much emphasis was put on how the US was entirely built by immigrants (anodised thanksgiving narratives, notwithstanding), in so doing, erasing the fundamental role forced migration and slavery played in the forming of their national identity. (See W.E.B. DuBois' Black Reconstruction in America 1860-1880 for a comprehensive account of the role of the then recently liberated African American in the rebuilding of the US national psyche, somewhat ironic in view of its Civil Rights Movement).

[28] The so called Trojan Horse scandal consisted of twenty one schools in Birmingham that were accused of fostering an atmosphere of intimidation and attitudes that leant towards Islamic extremism. These claims were made in an interim report that was written by the former

Birmingham, UK. The scandal involved the discovery of alleged Islamic extremism in schools (that had a majority Muslim presence). This perfectly illustrated Gilroy's 'melancholic' call for civic unity and majoritarian conformity, whose underlying belief is that majority Muslim faith schools are 'un-British'.[29] As a result of the scandal, the outgoing coalition government promptly promoted a return to the teaching of (as yet, unexplained) 'British values' in schools and colleges [20].

Both of these examples show how pernicious the call for integration is when the metanarrative of a nation is inconsistently exclusive. What I mean here is that, as outlined earlier, the UK's national identity is already built on 'difference' and 'distinctiveness' with the established devolution of three of its Kingdoms and its approaching regional English devolution. The devolved Kingdoms actually argued for their 'difference' and 'distinctiveness' when they campaigned for devolution in the late 90s. Furthermore, it was Scotland's arguments for its 'difference' and 'distinctiveness' (read 'separateness') that almost won its referendum for *independence*. It would appear to be fork tongued to blame multiculturalism for highlighting 'difference' and 'distinctiveness' when these values of diversity seem to already lie at the heart of the *British* identity.

So, if we expect post-colonial immigrants to integrate into a cultural memory that excludes their historical and continuing cultural (and economic) contributions and derides their 'distinctiveness' (whilst openly applauding others'); can the political call for civic integration be considered genuine? How can there be 'intercultural dialogue' from the standpoint of the importance of the embedded nature of culture,[30] [21] without the crucial process of being *remembered* in a nation's cultural memory? [22][31] If we look

counterterrorism chief Peter Clarke, as part of a government inquiry that was led by the former education secretary, Michael Gove. However, Robin Bevan, a head teacher at Southend high school, reminded delegates at the Association of Teachers and Lecturers' conference on March 30th 2015 that core British values actually change over time. He said that he was also worried about how a "future right-wing government, or a partner in that government" might interpret and implement these 'core values' of British society, and that, "a more sensible, reasoned approach to values" was needed.

[29] Within the context of a long British tradition of Christian faith schools.

[30] Bhikhu Parekh sees multiculturalism as consisting of three elements: the recognition of everyday cultural embeddedness and how it affects us all, the genuine desire for intercultural dialogue and cultural diversity and finally, the recognition that individual and distinct cultures are themselves porous, internally plural and dynamic. Parekh's description of multiculturalism seems to accurately characterise our national debates about Britishness within the political context of devolution.

[31] Even though we have UK Black History month in October, which very effectively archives historical black achievement and contribution to UK history, the fact that this activity is

at how this psyche of selective cultural memory manifests itself in purely socio-economic terms[32] [23], we actually see that failed policies around education [24], housing and job-creation [25] seem to have more to do with what many see as the primary flaw in multiculturalism, namely apparent ethnic 'separatism', than with any multicultural policies. This view is supported by Deborah Phillips' [26] research into the ethnic tensions in Bradford, UK:

> The construction of minority ethnic segregation as a 'problem' and British Muslims as alien, inward-looking 'Others' perpetuates, and indeed normalizes, the view that the responsibility for community tensions lies principally with the 'self-segregating' minorities. Yet the evidence from this research suggests that the radicalization of space in Bradford speaks more loudly of white control and bounded choices, both past and present. (pp. 36-37)

Here, Phillips strongly intimates that if we were to actually take note of Will Kymlicka's suggestion of acknowledging historic (and ongoing structural) injustices done to minorities, we would be able to better move away from blaming them for the structural inequalities in which they find themselves. Furthermore, I would argue that by *not* recognising the historical effects of structural inequality we *dehumanise* or fetishise communities, as they become *objects* of blame for their situations[33] [27]. I will unpack this process of dehumanisation later in the chapter when discussing Islamophobia. Internationally, this predicament of having to ask for what should be inalienable rights [28][34] is even more profound for what Kymlicka describes as indigenous peoples.

For me, talk of (ideological) multiculturalism implies a process of integration that is deemed only necessary for minorities that are presumed to not already have an integral stake in a national consciousness or a monistic

---

only officially celebrated for one month in the year and is not properly embedded in the National Curriculum that is taught year round, risks the appearance of tokenism. I say this because the enormous archival efforts of Black History month have not been embedded in the national institutionalised psyche of British identity, which is why the language and indeed the thinking behind current discussion around immigration can sometimes appear to be racist or xenophobic at the very least!

[32] James Kirkup finds that 'separatism' is more dependent on economics than on values and cites the relatively poor educational standards in many Muslim communities that prevent some community members from moving away into more 'diverse' areas.

[33] Or as Claire Alexander would call it the, "fetishization of marginality" (p.566)

[34] To adapt Thomas Jefferson's term of "unalienable" from the 1776 Declaration of Independence.

history. However, in the UK, I would argue that due to the *forgotten*[35] [29, 30, 31, 32], historical nation-building process of Empire, post-colonial immigrants were already integrated into the fabric of de facto UK history (as ably demonstrated by Black History Month's considerable archives) when they first arrived (many were already here, of course). However, they were later denied equal citizenship that should have been inherently assumed.[36] Similarly, around the world, indigenous peoples already had histories and cultural practices particular to their lands and societal identities that existed before European re-settlement moreover, they were the custodians of cultural land-practices that shaped the very nature of the mostly violent phases of foreign re-settlements and ensuing nation-building. To anodise these accounts of historical trauma done to indigenous peoples is to erase the memory of their contribution to that country's nation building[37] [33, 34]. If we briefly consider

---

[35] David Olusoga presents University College London's (UCL) research about the forgotten history of African chattel slavery on the British Isles and in the Caribbean. Via the 1834 census for the Slave Compensation Commission, £17bn (in modern money) of compensation (representing the immense wealth generated by this now national economy built on the sugar trade) was paid to "the owners of those slaves, by the British taxpayer, for the loss of their "property"". Olusoga and his team discovers how widely spread and mundane slavery was in the UK. The research discovers that it was not just large landowners who had slaves but

[m]any… middle-class slave owners had just a few slaves, possessed no land in the Caribbean and rented their slaves out to landowners, in work gangs. These bit-players were home county vicars, iron manufacturers from the Midlands and lots and lots of widows.

UCL research goes on to trace how the profits gained from the compensation built the modern physical and economic infrastructure of Britain and it also traces how the (racist) propaganda war waged by the then pro slavery lobby helped to shape the psyche of Britain's national institutions.

For example, the ideas of the hugely influential writer, Edward Long, who in his 1774 book, *The History of Jamaica, Volume 2*, famously cited Africans as being, "devoid of genius" and who "seem almost incapable of making any progress in civility or science. They have no plan or system of morality among them" (p. 353), formed the template for a British cultural memory that had embedded within it notions of polygenism. These racial characterisations pre-date similar US cultural memories by around a hundred years, if we read W.E.B Du Bois' *Black Reconstruction in America 1860-1880*. In her *Race in the US: Know your history*, A'Lelia Bundles also gives an excellent account of America's 'forgotten' historical struggles with race (especially in school curricula, and how this amnesia shapes the nation c.f. Du Bois). She argues that it is vitally important to *un-forget*, if the US' contemporary struggles around African American rights are to be fully understood and properly addressed.

[36] Many post-colonial immigrants regarded the UK as the Mother country and were in fact initially legally accepted as British citizens until their numbers grew and consequently frightened the government into restricting their access by rescinding the British citizen status of future incoming post-colonial migrants.

[37] Very much creating a Baudrillardian fourth level simulacra – a cultural mirage. However, in terms of economics, Daron Acemoglu et al. write how the mortality rates of early European settlers helped them to found two types of states. Firstly 'extractive states' where there was

our sub-state nationals in the UK, we can see that due to their remembered, valorised and sometimes bloody histories, there has never been a question of their national (political or ideological) civic integration or 'distinctiveness' (from a British perspective, at least[38]) only questions about the extent to which they can determine themselves.

As discussed, there is a great need for the curating of the cultural memory of a nation to be on-going in order to acknowledge all aspects of its history that will allow for a priori cultural membership. Since cultural memory for a nation (or its majorities) is about deciding who are members sharing its national psyche (and therefore are stakeholders) and who are not, this synthetic cultural narrative adopts the role of 'habitus'. Apart from its self-legitimising powers of taste (law) making, Pierre Bourdieu [35] defines habitus as being able to use its embedded historical traditions, even those that are 'forgotten', to govern its present and to dictate its future. Here, I am deliberately evoking Walter Benjamin's [36] shell imprint analogy[39] [37, 38], as it is the erased post-colonial and indigenous struggle against similarly erased (or mostly embedded) historically oppressive majoritarian traditions that hail political multiculturalism into being in a Butlerian sense[40] [39, 40, 41, 42, 43, 44]. The

high settler mortality and where institutions did not protect private property rights or guard against excessive government misappropriation because their, "main purpose...was to transfer as much of the resources of the colony to the colonizer, with the minimum amount of investment possible" (p. 1370). The second type of state is called a, "Neo-Europe" where settler mortality was relatively low and where "[t]he settlers tried to replicate European institutions, with great emphasis on private property, and checks against government power" (p. 1370). Acemoglu et al. argue that the type of institutions that were originally set up in the colonies continue to exist today and their institutional structures correlate to present day per capita economic wealth and performance. This economic point is of extreme significance to both present day indigenous and post-colonial migration and nation building.

38 Although Scottish, Northern Irish and Welsh nationalists might have a different view of what constitutes their integration.

39 Paradoxically, post-colonial and indigenous minorities are actually made more visible/present by their erasure from a nation's cultural memory. If we keep in mind, Walter Benjamin's description of (post)modernity as, "not being in a house but being in a shell [where] the shell bears the impression of its inhabitant[s]" (p. 220), we find that it is this imprint (on (post)modernity) of the historically erased that is actually made more visible (palpable). The imprint is made more visible through the social inequalities that political multiculturalism is meant to address. I am, of course, also borrowing from Homi K Bhabha's (via Frantz Fanon) post-colonial concept of identification and self-declaration via absence/erasure; a liminal space where the subject occupies a position of existence and non-existence at the same time. See Chapter 4 for a fuller analysis of this Benjaminesque "imprint".

40 It is interesting to note here that in the UK we do not seem to have an iconic non-subaltern author of the status of Germany's Günter Grass who embraced his nation's past and fully examined it. Although Miranda Carter points to Philip Hensher and William Dalrymple as notable exceptions, she acknowledges that the full complexities of the UK's Colonial past and identity still have not been embraced by the British psyche. Even the popular TV

key point about thinking of cultural memory as an agent of habitus in constructing a national consciousness is its very dynamic post-modern *powers* of arbitrary but universally accepted (Simmelian) self-invention. Cultural memory is therefore a living and organic, ongoing hegemony that institutionalises its own mythology, a simulation which often includes the misappropriation of contemporary ideas and their erroneous 'sale' as history, at will *and* with impunity.

## Multiculturalism As Defining Stakeholdership

So, it would seem that, perhaps the most important element of ideological multiculturalism is the formation of *stakeholdership*[41] [45, 46, 47, 48]. The concept of stakeholdership could be a more helpful way of examining ideological multiculturalism. Being a stakeholder implies a horizontal dialogue

dramatisations of British Colonial rule in India such as the 1984 TV adaptation of Paul Scott's novel The Jewel in the Crown, and the more recent 2015 TV drama Indian Summers by Paul Rutland seem not to have inspired genuine introspection. Not even Susanna Clarke's period fantasy novel (and its 2015 TV adaptation) Jonathan Strange and Mr Norrell that depicts nineteenth century Englishness through 'Blackness'/Otherness or Amma Asante's 2014 film Belle exploring the role of Britain in abolishing slavery, hit the mark for encouraging genuine introspection about British Colonial rule (identity). Nor its contemporary impact on immigration (despite their liminal Benjaminesque imprints).

[41] Here I am very much building on Bhikhu Parekh's "Pluralist Universalism" (p. 126) where:

…there are universal moral values and there is a creative interplay between them and the thick and complex moral structures of different societies, the latter domesticating and pluralizing the former and being in turn re-interpreted and revised in their light, thus leading to what I might call pluralist universalism. (p. 127)

See Chapter 3 for a more legalistic definition of this in terms of the basic and cultural dimensions of the articulation of "human dignity" within the framework of the Universal Declaration of Human Rights (UDHR). With Pluralist Universalism in mind, I am particularly exploring Parekh's sentiment that "a multicultural society cannot be stable and last long without developing a common sense of belonging among its citizens." (p. 341) This, of course, strongly echoes Ernest Renan's metaphor of a 'daily plebiscite', where I would suggest "a creative interplay between [universal moral values e.g., "human dignity"] and the thick and complex moral structures of …societies" cannot happen with agency before the stakeholdership of all societies' citizens is fully examined. Renan's 'daily plebiscite' could be read as describing the negotiation of stakeholdership as a process of continually looking into our shared histories to inform our present and strengthening our desire to continue to work and live together. See Chapter 1, for a fuller discussion about the different ethical models of citizenisation, including why this stakeholdership thesis profoundly disagrees with David Miller's Liberal Nationalism approach with its proposal of (tacit) civic integration contracts and a liberal minimum. As I will argue later, Miller's notion of 'deserts' reduces the individual to a state agent of civic unity who is rewarded with civic rights rather than an autonomous human being with inherent human rights (see note 52).

between equals (who have an equal historical and cultural stake) rather than a vertical hierarchy between majority stakeholders (with full civic entitlements) and minority non-stakeholder-'others' (with only partial or no civic entitlements for which they need to apply). Post-colonial and indigenous minorities who are not perceived to be stakeholders in a nation's self-defined narrative seem to be forced to need to adopt a somewhat post-modern majoritarian psyche in order to gain equal civic rights. This form of post-modern amnesia appears to be a key function of the neoliberal agenda where both Engelsian isolation and Simmelian re-invention falls to the atomised individual who needs to transform themselves to fit a synthetic account of a national history, a national history out of which they have been erased and find themselves without stake. So, what would better incentivise the 'individual' to try to fit into a majoritarian collective, than having a stake in such a collective?[42]

In her research into citizenisation ceremonies for successful applicants, Bridget Byrne [49] discovered that cultural memory plays an important part of 'constituting' the national stakeholder. Although this could sound like I am describing a form of interculturalism within a super-diverse [50] environment, in terms of my implied emphasis on cultural dialogue, the important difference is the a priori status of the stakeholder, which includes understanding what their stake is (thus needing to recognise their inherent stakeholder status). If a more *inclusive* cultural memory could be formed (and kept malleable) for a nation where minority historical claims of stakeholdership were acknowledged then *ideological* civic integration would become more about political *power sharing*, as it is with sub-state nationals rather than about political *power acquisition.* Without this working out of an a priori acknowledgement of stakeholdership, ideological multiculturalism still risks falling prey to the inherent social inequalities of neoliberalism.

## The Role of Myth in a Creating a US-led International Cultural Memory

Nowhere, is the issue around stakeholdership more keenly felt than by contemporary Muslim communities in the global context of terror and

---

[42] I am implying a version of the "Politics of Respectability", which I will later discuss in the US context.

radicalisation.[43] In this section, I will use as an example, the British rise of Islamophobia and its origins in an international cultural memory to illustrate the emergent differences between human and civic rights. Using the distinction between human and civic rights as a background context, I will also discuss the wider implications of Islamophobia for us all.

As introduced at the start of this chapter, the 2001 US, the 2005 UK terrorist attacks and the 2011 riots marked watershed moments in the forming of cultural memories and of national identities. For the first time in recent years, culture became a political tool of control and of global military projection alongside its equally powerful 'soft' global commercial forms.[44] These attacks sparked a Western response, arguably led by the US that became known as the 'war on terror'. What is striking here, is the literal militarisation of "culture" that is being used to enforce its own and distinct (self-referential) globally dominant political ideology. To date, the West led by the US appears to have been greatly influenced by the ideas in Samuel Huntington's book, *The Clash of Civilizations and the Remaking of the World Order*[45] [51, 52]. Huntington's central claim is that world power is essentially concentrated into discrete civilisations that are historically culture-bound to form monisms and such monisms throughout history have and indeed continue to clash for global supremacy. Huntington maintains that the 'civilisation' built on Islam is currently violently clashing with the 'civilisation' built on Western ideologies (or by inference Christianity). Even though Huntington's evaluation seems to ignore the historical and present interdependencies, porousness and fluidity of so called 'civilisations' (meaning that 'civilisations'/empires have always been plural), his claims, have nevertheless, allowed the West to fashion its latest cultural memory or myth of itself [53][46] into a political ideology that justifies its projection of current military and economic global dominance.

---

[43] A contested term that I will explore later.

[44] See Chapter 4 for the role of culture in globalisation.

[45] Expanded from his earlier article, Clash of Civilizations.

[46] Cynthia Weber reminds us of the extreme importance that myth and storytelling have in our sense-making of the world especially from our post-modern perspectives. Weber gives an excellent breakdown of the current myths that underpin the curation of cultural memory and our international political frameworks. These myths are; 'Realism' where nations compete for their own interests without a 'world orderer'; creating anarchy. 'Idealism' where nations compete for their interests in cooperation with each other, forming an international community; creating order. 'Constructivism' where nations decide for themselves what 'anarchy' or 'order' is and act likewise. 'Gender' where gender is a compartmentalised additional variable (or is it intersectionally embedded in the formation of cultural memory? This question could also be asked for race). 'Globalisation' where there is a global influence and control of Western ideologies, including economic and financial mechanisms. 'Neo-Marxism' where there is the global economic substructure; the new 'world orderer' acting

Huntingdon's ideas have allowed the West to culturally re-invent its history and its values based on its own reckoning of its geopolitical position. By fashioning a new cultural memory that uses fear (of Islamist terror) to help sell the contemporaneous ideas of freedom and democracy as historical traditions, the West has been able to export its global brand of "civilisation" with not a cry of *civic* unity but of *humanitarian* unity. This call for humanitarian unity was most clearly crystallised by George Bush's [54] now famous quote, "You're either with us or against us in the fight against terror." As numerous commentators have already noted at great length, the war on terror (and before that, the Cold War) has used fear to mythologise a western fantasy of freedom that perhaps never really existed. The grand defence of (Western) freedom(s) as an international guiding light has become a 'melancholic' call of humanitarian unity in the sense Gilroy attributed to Britain, in this case, now arguably referring to America's 'vanishing pre-eminence'. Here, I specifically mean that if we take the US, as the international leader of this 'melancholic' call, we can see that its own claims of historical guardianship of the values of freedom and democracy are far from convincing. We only need to look at the history of its own Civil Rights Movement and the legacy of its modern-day denials of civic and *human* rights.

This is important to consider because in 1948, the Universal Declaration of Human Rights (UDHR), which can be viewed as an important cornerstone of US and international myth-making around freedom and democracy (along with the US' Bill of Rights in the Declaration of Independence), was written in the shadow of World War II to prevent the re-occurrence of wartime atrocity. However, it would appear that not all atrocities carried out against human life were at the time, counted as equal. During this period of international humanitarian concern, African Americans (who also fought for the very (western) freedoms and democracy supposedly won by the war!) were still subject to the often brutal and sometimes fatal Jim Crow laws of the Southern States.[47] The US chair of the UDHR, Eleanor Roosevelt would have been keenly aware of this at the time. Paul Gilroy [55] and Carol Elaine Anderson [56] remind us that nowhere in the genesis of the UDHR did the thinking even

behind the scenes, building an unseen 'empire'? And finally, 'Modernisation and Development Theory' where there are different cultures vying for supremacy, the cause of global conflict?

[47] See Chapter 3 for a full discussion about the role of "human dignity" as a marker of fundamental human rights, something the Jim Crow laws ignored. This is also hugely ironic as the Republic of South Africa abstained from voting for the adoption of the UDHR, to protect its own version of Jim Crow, namely Apartheid – where black South Africans were also not apparently counted as human beings with human rights.

consider the post-slavery and reconstruction journey of a peoples whose (initially forced) labour helped to shape the nation of the then emerging world leader and chair of this international humanitarian initiative.

What we had was a Benjaminesque imprint of absence where the fact that African Americans were not considered stakeholders in their own nation's psyche meant that a universal declaration of human rights (ostensibly led by the US to ensure freedom and democracy for all) seemed hollow. We need to remember that at this time, not all African Americans even had the right to vote, especially in the southern states[48] [57, 58]. This is what Malcolm X [59] alluded to in his 1964 Manhattan speech at the *Founding Rally of the Organization of Afro-American Unity* when he called for the Human Rights (not the Civil Rights) of the African American to be recognised[49] [60]. So, apart from the international abstentions, it would appear then, from at least a US perspective, the rights of human beings were, in fact, not universal but rather selective, limited to only those who were counted as stakeholders in their nation's cultural memory. The link between the denial of (universal) human rights to certain domestic communities and this selective international 'universality' being adopted only by others willing to become stakeholders in the forging of a Western (international) cultural memory has been brought to the fore by scholars such as Riffat Hassan [61], (p. 25) who states that:

> What needs to be pointed out to those who uphold the Universal Declaration of Human Rights to be the highest, or sole, model, of a charter of equality and liberty for all human beings, is that given the Western origin and orientation of this Declaration, the "universality" of the assumptions on which it is based is - at the very least - problematic and subject to questioning[50] [62, 63].

---

[48] Even though the 1870 15th Amendment to the Constitution gave African American men the right to vote, this was not consistently upheld (in the south) until President Lyndon Johnson, in 1965 convinced Congress to pass legislation that enforced the voting rights that were enshrined in 15th Amendment. This voting-rights legislation was extended and given greater powers in 1970, 1975 and 1982. Elsewhere, I argue that, amongst other things, Obama's two terms as President were meant to have played a symbolic role in addressing both the internal and external perceptions of African American stakeholdership in the US.

[49] A point echoed by Martin Luther King in spirit if not in words in his 1963 I Have a Dream speech he made in Washington when he mentioned how the African American had been given a "bad cheque" unable to cash the "unalienable rights" promised to them by Thomas Jefferson.

[50] If we acknowledge Kymlicka's contention that multiculturalism is based on the human rights revolution, even the universalisation of human rights can still be regarded, to a certain degree, as an oversimplification of the human cultural condition along the lines of the

Here, Hassan implies that the inherent contradiction of a self-referential Western 'universal' humanitarian myth that was founded on omission[51] was used to construct an international and post-modern cultural memory, à la Nora, with all of the synthetic hallmarks of a Huntingdon-like (monistic) "civilization." Furthermore, this 'civilisation', founded on supposedly 'universal values' awarded itself law (taste) making powers of habitus,[52] which in turn, today, allows it to choose who is, "either with us or against us."

## Islamophobia and Multiculturalism in the UK

It is this habitus that is expressed dichotomously as being, "either with us or against us" (in or out), that has allowed the Huntingdon clash of civilisations myth to really take hold in the psyche of the 'international community'[53] [64, 65, 66, 67, 68]. It could also be said that it is this habitus or

---

previously discussed monistic storytelling. What I specifically mean here is that without not only a concept of an a priori stakeholdership (on which the human rights movement is supposedly based) but also an ongoing process of integrating and developing cultural memories, capable of meaningfully expressing that equal stakeholdership (both temporally and globally), this process of citizenisation risks becoming a means of pernicious Foucauldian control. It becomes a control that is designed to subjugate (and homogenise) instead of to liberate (and heterogenise). This point is richly explored by Alison Dundes Renteln in her book, International Human Rights: Universalism Versus Relativism. She reminds us that by the invitation of the 1947 Commission on Human Rights (CHR), the American Anthropologists Association advised the CHR that it was not possible to have a universal set of human rights based only on Western values without the declaration becoming an ethnocentric document. Renteln cites that the CHR ignored this advice, whilst finalising the Declaration by lawyers not by anthropologists.

[51] See note 26 about liminal space.

[52] See Chapter 3 for a fuller discussion on the ethics of International Law and Human Rights.

[53] The myth of an 'international community' as proposed by Charles Kegley (via Kenneth Waltz) is contentious because it is an assumed state of reality with an a priori sense of stakeholdership for its members (i.e., it is in everyone's best interests to join in order to avoid international anarchy). However, other readings of this 'reality' describe less of an international community and more of a domestication of the international space by the US. This is where nations adopt a cultural memory that is Americocentric, at the risk of diluting their own unique national perspectives – a cultural effect of (hierarchical) globalisation that forces nations to give up their own cultural memories in order to become stakeholders in an 'international community' with underlying pretensions of becoming a "civilisation". Steve Smith gives an excellent account of the US' dominance of thinking in the field of International Relations Theory that belies the concept of an international community. Paradoxical and hugely ironic, if the 'international community' is actually nothing more than a domesticated Americocentric space (a global extension of US national boundaries), then the idea of a universal set of rights and freedoms (initially modelled on US values), turns the West's much vaunted democracy-led evangelism into a benign autocracy (at its most optimistic!) Interestingly, even Michael Hardt & Antonio Negri's observation that,

new(ish) consensus of 'international community' that is keeping Orientalism[54] [69], alive with a vengeance. If we take stock of who is in the "coalition of the willing"[55] [70] and who is not and more importantly, which Muslim states are in and those who are out, we will be able to plainly see that there is an 'international' concept of 'good Muslim' and 'bad Muslim'. In other words, those Muslims 'we cannot work with' and those with whom we can in order to further our Western geopolitical interests [70]. We can observe Orientalism at work in how the 'good Muslims' are given special dispensation to carry on with their 'exotic' practices[56] as long as they are able to comply with their responsibilities as stakeholders in the international 'community'. However, the extent to which they are considered bona fide stakeholders in this international cultural memory or (synthetic) 'civilisation' is unclear.

The traditional monism of the national state seems to have given way to a transnational monism of the 'international community', and can be used as an example of how the (US) domestication of the international space has the potential to reconstruct the internal cultural memories of individual nation states into a composite image of 'Empire' or 'Civilisation'. A case in point can be found in Steven Vertigans' [72] paper, which illustrates how the hegemonic 'war on terror' is shaping the UK's national thinking about Islam and its perceived threats. Vertigans describes how an Orientalism[57] that is hailed into being performatively in the UK, through underlying cultural narratives/tropes around the "exotic" and "savage Arab" represents a lack of stakeholdership in

---

"[f]irst and foremost, then, the concept of Empire posits a regime that effectively encompasses the spatial totality, or really that rules over the entire ''civilized'' world." (p. xiv) sounds suspiciously to me like a domesticated 'international' cultural memory (space), as previously discussed. Despite their protestations to the contrary and their advocacy of a diffuse Foucauldian power matrix (see note 50), they tellingly acknowledge that the Empire indeed has influence over the "civilised" world. This notion of the "civilised" in terms of necessarily determining what is civilised and what is not, not only suggests an Orientalist view but fits Bourdieu's notion of habitus very well. This is especially the case when they further invoke its law (taste) making powers with, "[f]rom the perspective of Empire, this is the way things will always be and the way they were always meant to be. In other words, Empire presents its rule not as a transitory moment in the movement of history, but as a regime with no temporal boundaries and in this sense outside of history or at the end of history." (pp. xiv-xv)

[54] Against which Edward Said so influentially railed.

[55] Jesse Lorenz gives a good account of who the "coalition of the willing" is and what their economic and geopolitical motivations are for joining the coalition.

[56] The differences between Islamic traditions are often homogenised into an 'exotic' (in a dangerous sense) "Other" in popular consciousness or cultural memory. Tolerating Islam in this case then becomes merely a form of pragmatism based on the promise of self-gain not mutual trust.

[57] In this instance where 'many complicated strands are reduced to a simple tale of essential and enduring international unity.'

the UK's cultural psyche (memory), which in turn threatens 'British values' (ideological multiculturalism). In the UK, this form of Orientalism is referred to as Islamophobia and is targeted at Muslim communities.

Vertigans argues that this national cultural memory is progressively manifesting itself in its domestic anti-terror legislation and media representation[58] [73, 74], of Muslim communities (political multiculturalism). The irony of this is that the very freedoms and equalities that political multiculturalism is meant to bring are being eroded by an ideological form of 'multiculturalism' that entails orientalising Muslim communities in so doing, not recognising their *a priori* stakeholdership in the nation's (original) cultural memory. It is as though their historical post-colonial contribution to the UK's cultural memory has been erased and replaced with a new international cultural memory built on a synthetic call for *humanitarian* unity (against the fear of terror). Nora would characterise this as a very post-modern Western tendency to historicise the present to the detriment of the past. I would go further to add that this tendency is a key function of Simmelian neoliberal self-invention built on the consumerisation of cultural memory.[59] Vertigans observes that the hyper and mass-surveillance, the targeted stop and searches (political multiculturalism embodying Foucauldian juridical power) and the group stigmatisation of the majority by the few (ideological multiculturalism embodying Foucauldian discipline power) amongst many other 'othering' factors, serve to *dehumanise* and pathologise[60] [75] Muslim communities into *objects* of state control, suspicion and blame, as previously outlined. We can see that by reducing Muslims to a homogenous block of "good Muslims" who pose no internal threat, as opposed to "bad Muslims" who are 'radicalised'[61]

[58] I suppose here I am implying an Althusserian state apparatus. Amir Saeed, Rusi Jaspal & Marco Cinnirella write at great length about how the 'Muslim threat' to British identity and security appears to be greatly exaggerated in the media.

[59] With Tavia Nyong'o's "Participation as a Neoliberal Fantasy" in mind!

[60] Mehdi Hasan writes movingly about the personal consequences of being perceived as a British non-stakeholder Muslim and how this process of dehumanisation affects his family and friends. See note 71 for the process of pathologisation of Muslim communities. Also see Chapter 3 for a full discussion about the effects of dehumanisation on the concept of "human dignity" and Human Rights.

[61] Charlotte Heath-Kelly cogently explains that the "radicalisation" discourse in the UK is far from settled as the exact nature of radicalisation is still unknown (at what point does one become radicalised and how?) It is also worth noting in this context that John Horgan & Max Taylor's research points to a lack of correlation between being a 'radical' and being a terrorist (not all radicals are terrorists nor all terrorists, radicals). This means that within the UK's (anti-terrorist) PREVENT strategy, Muslims occupy a liminal position of being 'at risk' (of radicalisation) and being 'risky' (radicalised). However, Heath-Kelly implies that even being 'at risk' (i.e., being vulnerable) by extension means that Muslims are still perceived as being 'risky' (the underlying thinking is that if Muslims are perceived to have

[75, 77], and pose a national threat, we are witnessing a process where Muslims are no longer considered heterogeneous autonomous human beings with an a priori stake in nationhood. We then constitute them as mere agents whose homogenous state-encouraged actions *might possibly earn* them national stakeholdership (if they are good enough and show that they are "with us"). Here, we have an example of how one post-colonial minority occupies a liminal space of being seen and not seen simultaneously, as their *humanity* is erased and is replaced by the role of *agent* of national interest (i.e., internal security, making international membership possible). Brian David Jacobs [78] writes extensively about the UK's post-colonial African Caribbean minorities' historical struggle for their civic rights in the 50's and 60's. However, their "othering" and corresponding processes of dehumanisation (e.g., disproportionate stop and searches[62] [79, 80, 81]), are not directly related to the international cultural memory because their citizenship poses no threat to the UK's geopolitical interests.

So my original question in this chapter; precisely into what are (post-colonial) minorities expected to integrate, remains important. If we accept (ideological) multiculturalism on a national level as a call for *civic* unity[63] [82, 83], in view of the current treatment of Muslim communities (and others) in the UK, are we actually saying that ideological multiculturalism is in reality, only contingent on how well its *agents* perform their role in maintaining or achieving civic unity? I say this because without an a priori acknowledgement of (heterogeneous) stakeholdership in a nation's cultural memory, minorities are therefore forced to *earn* their stakeholdership but only as homogenised de-humanised 'Others', performing their duties and responsibilities as mere agents of unity.

## Human Rights vs. Civic Rights?

If multiculturalism is to be viewed as both an ideological view of stakeholdership and a political process of citizenisation, I see two categories of

no a priori stake then their vulnerability will make them more likely to become radicalised). This in effect, casts all Muslims under the suspicion of being a potential threat to the state.

[62] Due to their supposed inherently hyper-violent tendencies, also as represented by their equally disproportionate representation in the penal system.

[63] But as part of a synthetic call for humanitarian unity forming an international cultural memory that rules with the combination of powers resembling Bourdieu's habitus (taste (law) making 'field') and Foucault's juridical (institutional prohibition and punishment), discipline (social norming) and bio (population management) powers.

citizens emerging from this conceptual framework. One type of citizen is primarily regarded as a human being (with 'inalienable' rights) and has a priori stakeholdership and is seen as a citizen (with civic rights) as a consequence of their primary stakeholder-status, which means crucially, not having to prove citizenship.[64] The other type of citizen is merely regarded as a state-sanctioned agent who has to first *prove* their good citizenship for the good of the state[65] [84, 85, 86], before they can be regarded as a citizen (with civic rights) but significantly, not having a priori stakeholdership means that inherent ('inalienable') human rights are not guaranteed to them. Essentially, this second type of citizen is at best, given only a case-by-case form of pragmatic a posteriori stakeholdership dependent on behaviour judged "good" by the state habitus. As multiculturalism is part of the human rights movement, itself somewhat incomplete in its universal application, this *performative* act of citizenisation via ideological multiculturalism is significant because it determines to whom both 'inalienable' human *and* civic rights are given and also to whom only civic rights are given.

---

[64] Like our sub-national minorities who do not need to earn their national stakeholdership due to their non-'Othered' autonomous and heterogeneously assumed humanity (as citizens) that already accords them a priori stakeholder status.

[65] As epitomised by the "good Muslim"/"bad Muslim" narrative, (analogous to Liberal Nationalism and the notion of 'deserts', see note 28 and Chapter 1) or today's economic migrant from Eastern Europe. Although the Eastern European economic migrant is also not regarded as a stakeholder, they are accorded inherent human and civic rights. They gain these rights by virtue of their membership (stakeholdership) of the European Union with its Free Movement laws (a distinct subset of the "international community" with its own cultural memories that are enshrined in its various treaties), even though xenophobic (and racist) rhetoric would only just accord them civic rights, if given half a chance! In fact, pushing this thought to its extreme, John Holmwood & Gurminder Bhambra critique Eric Posner & Glen Weyl's ideas around the "freedom of movement of unfree labour" (modelled on Qatar), where non EU migrant workers would be prevented from establishing a sense of "belonging" to their host country. Posner & Weyl argue that institutionalising non-stakeholdership would make it easier for governments to pay migrants drastically less than the lowest local wages in return for 'residence' in that country, arguing that life as an (in effect) 'indentured' worker would still be better than their previous lives. Their central argument is that by allowing migrant workers to work for less than the local wages it would help to balance the economic deficit between the Global North and Global South, as the wages received by the migrants would be sent back home to support their families! Holmwood & Bhambra characterise this as a "pro slavery argument". They argue that the situation in which these migrants find themselves is a result of current and historical geopolitical factors that the Global North has conveniently erased from its cultural memory but still needs to address directly by means other than "foreign aid". Holmwood & Bhambra propose that other strategies need to be used that acknowledge historical responsibility for current economic imbalances (not to mention that the Global South remains poor despite current similar (il)legal migrant working arrangements across the Global North!)

# ETHICAL IMPLICATIONS OF POLITICAL MULTICULTURALISM IN THE UK

In this context of the distinction between human and civic rights, ideological multiculturalism can be viewed purely in terms of creating a conceptual framework for deciding how to view (conceive of) subjects who are not recognised as sharing a stake in a nation's cultural memory.[66] If this is the case, then it follows that political multiculturalism becomes very much a process of citizenisation where what is really being described is how a non-stakeholding citizen is determined (then treated) in terms of their civic *function* of the state. In other words, what *benefit* is the subject to the state in terms of promoting civic unity, how do they *demonstrate* that benefit and under what circumstances can the state *recognise and reward* that benefit (their actions) with the granting of civic rights? I will now briefly outline the ethical considerations behind some of these political processes of citizenisation.

## The Politics of Respectability

One of the most striking examples of the difference between human and civic rights and the process of dehumanisation can be been in the US. As previously discussed, both Malcolm X and Martin Luther King observed that the African American was not regarded as a stakeholder in his/her country's cultural memory and as a result received neither human nor civic rights. So, as a non-stakeholder, the African American had to employ various strategies of proving her/his citizenship in order to gain civic rights. One such strategy was the 'Politics of Respectability', a term coined by *Evelyn Brooks-Higginbotham* [87] in her book *Righteous Discontent: The Women's Movement in the Black Baptist Church, 1880-1920. Brooks-Higginbotham describes how,* "[n]orthern white efforts, specifically those of the American Baptist Home Mission Society (ABHMS) and its women's auxiliaries in New England and the Midwest, played a seminal role in the development of educated black leaders" (p. 21). Education [88, 89, 90][67] was seen as a key to acquiring a kind of

[66] If Will Kymlicka's third principle of multiculturalism is not followed.

[67] Whether this was for the education of 'Negro' professionals and civic leaders for which W.E.B. Du Bois campaigned (via his 'Talented Tenth' strategy) or for a more inclusive vocational education that promoted self-sustainability and enterprise for which Booker T. Washington and Nannie Helen Burroughs advocated. However, L'Monique King makes the

'respectability' that would 'uplift' the African American to the same status of the White American. In addition to Education, a higher standard of morality was encouraged by the 'educated black [female] leaders'[68] with the help of the white women of the ABHMS. This was at a time when, "white society viewed black women as innately promiscuous and undeserving of protection from insult and even rape" (p.100) – in other words, black women were denied the a priori *human right* to dignity![69] [91] So, it was seen as the sole responsibility of the Negro to change their ways and to emulate (at that time) white Victorian middle class sensibilities (majoritarian bias) in order to earn equality as fellow citizens (stakeholders) - a ruthless and pernicious form of 'discipline' power.[70]

To this day, the 'Politics of Respectability' persists in the educational form of what John Ogbu [92] characterises as the "Burden of Acting White," where he observes black students code-switching and adopting different speech patterns and vernaculars in order to fit in with their white peers[71] [93]. However, Mychal Denzel Smith [94] and Kali N. Gross [95] amongst others[72] [96] strongly denounce the failure of the 'Politics of Respectability', to challenge structural inequality. They argue that African Americans should not need to adopt a strategy of assimilation in order to earn their civic or human

point that although both aspirations being two sides of the same coin, were equally worthy at the turn of the twentieth century, today's educational achievement gap between blacks and whites in the US seems as wide as ever due to the prevalence of an unofficial segregated education system. King argues that education of the individual is not enough in itself to change structural inequality. This is also a point statistically made by William R. Emmons & Bryan J. Noeth in their report for the Federal Reserve Bank of St Louis, Why Didn't Higher Education Protect Hispanic and Black Wealth?

[68] Brooks-Higginbotham documents the extreme importance of the intersectional struggles that the female black Baptists, especially the 'Female Talented Tenth', endured in order to secure racial 'uplift' for both men and women.

[69] I make this point in the sense of inherent human dignity, as 'human dignity' had not yet been codified into the Universal Declaration of Human Rights, as it didn't yet exist. Contemporary writer and social activist Ida B Barnett-Wells in her recollections, *On Lynchings* admits that even the white women of the ABHMS didn't quite escape the lack of human dignity accorded their black charges with being called, "Nigger Teachers" whilst being, "insulted, persecuted and ostracised, not by Negroes, but by the white manhood which boasts of its chivalry towards women" (p. 38)

[70] See note 50.

[71] Elsewhere, I write at length how the 'Politics of Respectability' within education is transformed into the 'work harder' ethic and the secret US curriculum of militarianism for the African American working classes, where the responsibility for effecting change is placed on the individual instead of the system. This naturally creates a successful elite at the expense of the failed masses – very much a neo-liberal construct.

[72] E. Patrick Johnson & Mae G Henderson give a great account of how the 'politics of respectability' is especially important to the intersectionality of Black Queer studies.

rights and that this strategy is still not preventing sometimes fatal structural inequalities, especially regarding state law enforcement[73] [97, 98].

A similar process of citizenisation occurred in the UK over fifty years later but with a crucial difference; this process of assimilation was enacted at the state level through immigration policy rather than at the individual grass roots level [99]. Britain's process of assimilation also illustrated its "melancholic attachment to its vanished pre-eminence" with its performative post-colonial phenomenon of "Black" homogenising whose dehumanising effects would later create liminal anomalies of representation.

## Assimilation

Heidi Mirza [100] identifies this era as being represented by Enoch Powell's 1968 *Rivers of Blood speech* [101]. The former MP for Wolverhampton Southwest expressed a supposedly national fear of the White British citizen being deluged by immigrants leading to what he quoted from Virgil [102] as being like the, "[r]iver Tiber foaming with much blood" (6.86). The largely Afro-Caribbean (West Indian) and South Asian immigrants at the time were, "deemed culturally, socially and intellectually inferior, coming from uncivilized parts of the world" [103] (p. 12). From an ideological view point, this notion of being "uncivilized" is a prime example of how the post-colonial history of the immigrants was erased from the British psyche – very perplexing, as many of these immigrants under British rule in the former colonies had enjoyed (or endured!) the educational and legal traditions of the Mother Country. Even though, initially, the government of the day had legally recognised the new immigrants as equal citizens (under 'Citizen of the UK and the Colonies' status) and had even passed the 1968 Race Relations Bill designed to counter discrimination (political multiculturalism), Powell's sentiments echoed the (ideological) importance of the need to recognise

---

[73] Of his #BlackLivesMatter community activism, born and bourne out of a response to the Michael Brown murder and subsequent state violence enacted against African Americans, Deray McKesson powerfully writes:

Naming this violence means one thing: the police and the state must change. It is not our job to shift the skin and identities into which we were born. It is up to systems of law enforcement, and the systems and structures that sustain its presence, to change.

Stafford Scott also writes about the impunity of the UK's police where an officer has yet to be convicted of the deaths of Cynthia Jarrett, Joy Gardner Roger Sylvester, Mark Duggan et. al. and the extreme lack of trust within local communities this engenders via bouts of social unrest.

stakeholdership. Powell believed that, "the [white British] citizen should not be denied to discriminate in the management of his private affairs between one fellow-citizen and another." For Powell, such a bill would only serve to protect the rights of the immigrants who did not want to integrate and in so doing discriminate against the white majority.

## The 'Benign' Institution[74]

Powell's thoughts clearly showed that for him discrimination should remain a personal affair and not be interfered with by the state. Following on from this, David Gillborn [104] makes the important point that when racism was actually acknowledged, it tended to be minimised in two significant ways; firstly, by focussing on 'individual' actions and secondly, by regarding these individual actions as temporally aberrant. Neither characterisation acknowledges the chronic and structural (institutional) nature of racism that permeates all aspects of everyday life [105, 106]. This fleeting and individually aberrant characterisation of racism could only be acknowledged as a 'fixed' concept because it did not allow for discussion of a form of racism that adapted to societal developments and was subtle and malleable in form. Although, Mirza [107, 108] calls this inability to examine the subtle, malleable and structural effects of racism as a new type of racism, I would argue that this was an older type of racism that characterised this period. Powell was only able to consider racism a personal affair precisely because of his (state-endorsed) ability to re-conceptualise the unacknowledged structural effects of discrimination as consisting of individual, cultural and religious (in terms of difference) 'failures' of ethnic minorities at a pathological level – the fetishsising of ethnic minorities into *objects* of blame. Gillborn [109] notes that racism within a White supremacist paradigm was marginalised within important debates on immigration and the integration of ethnic minorities because of what I would add, the prevalent popular belief in the 'benign' (or at worst, neutral) institution.

[74] From here, I will use the term "institution" as a generic term for civic as well as state organisations whose function is that of governance.

## The Tacitly 'Complicit' Institution

Even though the establishment made a huge show of denouncing Powell's speech, Ciarán Burke [110] reminds us that political multiculturalism in practice appeared to sympathise with Powell's ideological concerns. Burke outlines how the 1968 Immigration Act was tightened up to render the post-colonial immigrant status of 'Citizen of the UK and the Colonies' (which ideologically implied acknowledged stakeholdership) meaningless when "patrial" status was introduced. What patrial status meant was that post-colonial stakeholdership was only recognised if the entrant had a close blood relation or marital link to a Commonwealth citizen resident in the UK. So those post-colonial immigrants from Australia, New Zealand and Canada (white) were often given preference for UK entry (citizenship) over South Asian and Afro-Caribbean post-colonials (non-white). This was a case of political multiculturalism via its power of habitus, enacting a *racialised* erasure of stakeholdership in the UK's cultural memory, in so doing conforming to its ideological counterpart.

To facilitate integration into British society, political opinion of the time deemed it necessary for the newly arrived (non-white) post-colonials to adopt a working class 'Britishness' with a view towards minimising their original cultural traits and histories. This illustrates the dehumanising effect of ideological multiculturalism where without an acknowledged a priori stake, post-colonials had to trade their historical heterogeneity for a more controllable homogeneity in order to be given an a posteriori stake in Britain's cultural memory. In other words to be an effective agent of the state, with their rights contingent on their performance, post-colonials had to be re-constituted as "Black" to more easily fit into the majoritarian class system so that they could become politically and culturally acceptable. This manifested itself in a form of political multiculturalism where the various ethnic identities (and histories) that made up post-colonial Britain were encouraged to assemble in the then (national) Community Relations Boards. Although local councils would have argued the need for official (civic) spaces where they could work with representatives from the post-colonial communities, this in effect became a form of state-sponsored political "othering," where all of the various post-colonial cultures were homogenised into being "Black." It was here that Britain mirrored the US' Politics of Respectability because the various ethnic identities of the post-colonial communities adapted their own cultural traditions of hierarchy to the British class system. Brian David Jacobs colourfully describes the caste tensions between members of the Hindu and

Sikh communities where the higher castes would continue their homeland discrimination against the lower castes who, as a result, would ally themselves more closely to the British Trade Unions and the Indian Workers' Associations. Jacobs also notes that the West Indians integrated more easily than their South Asian counterparts because of their Christian religion and weaker community affiliations but this also caused tensions between the West Indian and South Asian communities, in addition to the ongoing internal tensions within the South Asian communities themselves.

Britain's lack of acknowledgement of (the contemporaneous impact of) its post-colonial history meant that the historical differences and ethnic tensions within the post-colonial communities were never really given the space to be explored and resolved within the context of national stakeholdership. This meant that post-colonials were always viewed with suspicion because these tensions and ethnic disunities were perceived as a lack of efficacy in carrying out their duties as state-sanctioned agents of civic unity[75] [111, 112]. In fact, the internal tensions between the post-colonial communities only served to underline their perceived pathological dysfunction (uncivilised natures), which permanently barred them from any sense of a priori stakeholdership in Britain's cultural memory.

Despite the political challenges that post-colonial communities faced in negotiating their civic rights, via their formation of grassroots organisations, they did continue to slowly mount more effective political campaigns with their alliances with political left-wing parties such as the Labour Party and the Trades Unions. However, the gradual expansion of this national 'black constituency' and their alliances with working class political parties encouraged the DES (Department for Education and Science), "to subsume the problems of immigrant minorities under those of the disadvantaged, and minimise any special help given to minorities" [113] (p. 67). In her important speech in 1978, Margaret Thatcher, the soon to be Prime Minister aired her concerns that the British people were, "really afraid that this country might be swamped by people of a different culture" [114]. This continuation of Enoch

[75] Helen Pidd writes about the antagonism between the South Asian, African and Caribbean communities in Bradford, where there seems to be an issue around a 'proximity to whiteness' that re-enforces 'caste prejudices' based on skin colour. Pidd's piece centres on the fatal stabbing of a Nigerian teacher by a Pakistani pupil due to this underlying antagonism. See Chapter 4 for a fuller discussion about the 'whiteness' and 'proximity to whiteness' discourse and its now market-led instead of race-led loci. These ethnic tensions, which are important for considering the conversion and integration of Black Muslims into the wider Muslim community, very much lay the ground for Charlotte Heath-Kelly's radicalisation discourse concept of "opacity". See note 73.

Powell's ideology is widely seen to have been a seminal moment in her journey to parliamentary victory a year later. Barry Troyna [115] suggests that this policy conflagration finally cemented the stripping away of the specific importance of race to multicultural policy.

## Civic Unity at What Cost?

If we zoom forward to London's 2012 Olympics, its epithet of "The World in a City" [116] was a powerful example of how a nation's cultural memory had evolved into apparently celebrating its welcomed super-diversity [117]. However, we do need to remember that this celebrated super-diversity still had not yet acknowledged the internal tensions of its post-colonial communities or their historical Colonial reasons. But what was interesting was how the ceremony nevertheless commoditised 'diversity' and gave it a literal market value.[76] Elsewhere, I write extensively about how cultural values, and in this case, embedded cultural values around diversity, can be given a market value and traded [118]. Here, Revathi Krishnaswarmy's sentiment that, "corporate globalization is thriving precisely by emptying out the subversive potential in culture" [119] (p. 108) is especially true. The London Olympics opening ceremony's parade of 'super-diversity' did not fully capture the tensions of a priori stakeholdership (i.e., examining its post-colonial heritage), as it presented an institutionally endorsed oversimplified narrative of, "essential and enduring national unity" [120] (p. 2.9, 16). So the historical and potentially subversive claims of a priori stakeholdership underpinning London's (and the UK's) super-diversity were never fully explained. In many respects, this spectacle was very much a market-led update on an earlier UK form of multiculturalism much derided by Yasmin Alibhai-Brown [121] called the 3S's - the now clichéd representation of multicultural diversity as represented by samosas, saris and steel bands.

[76] The economic benefits for the UK for hosting the Olympics. Again, the opportunity for the re-evaluation of Britain's cultural memory was traded for the market gain of hosting the Olympics, demonstrating Simmelian neoliberal self-invention.

## Early 3S Multiculturalism in the United Kingdom

"Tolerance, respect and an acceptance of collective identities" [122] (p. 1027) became a priority for political multiculturalism in the 80's and 90's in the UK:

> This [was] undertaken through supporting community associations and their cultural activities, monitoring diversity in the workplace, encouraging positive images in the media and other public spaces, and modifying public services (including education, health, policing and courts) in order to accommodate culture-based differences of value, language and social practice. (p. 1027)

This heightened visibility was yet another continuation of the "othering" process that was initiated during the era of assimilation. Since ideological multiculturalism was still no nearer to acknowledging a priori stakeholdership, it fell onto the political process of citizenisation to work out how to cope with 'difference' or how to legislate for the 'tolerance' of difference. In many respects, this was a profound move towards greater dehumanisation or fetishsisation of post-colonial communities. Instead of accepting the complexity (and heterogeneity) of their cultural diversity and critically assessing this in the context of shaping the British cultural memory, their differences were fetishsised and turned into exotic spectacles ostensibly for the pleasure of the majority. It was always going to be a huge ask of the majority to adopt legislated 'tolerance' if they were given no reason to 'tolerate' beyond the mere spectacle. Steven Vertovec [123] astutely notices that this type of multicultural discourse was always largely focussed on Afro-Caribbean and South Asian cultures to the exclusion of other less visible cultures or ethnic groups. Needless to say, this form of 'tolerance' did not signal any structural changes where racial discrimination was reduced, it merely swept these pressing issues under the carpet of 'carnival and celebration'.

Since post-colonials were homogenised as "Black," this became a form of institutionalised multi-ethnic acceptance, which served to turn the discourse into a black and white dichotomy (pre-empting the later equally dichotomous values-based "with us or against us" stance). Ideologically, this meant that it became easier to compartmentalise the multi-ethnic discourse in terms of black and white, where black was always regarded as the "exotic Other" that was to be displayed, performed and celebrated at the expense of examining the structured inequalities that allowed the exotic "Othering" to continue [124]. If we keep in mind the performative aspect of the process of citizenisation, 3S multiculturalism could also be seen as a literal 'performance' that post-colonials had to deliver in order to prove their civic worth. How far did the post-colonials have to go in performing (in the Butlerian sense too) stereotypes of themselves in order to be accepted as equal citizens? Moreover, in the absence of the acknowledgement of a priori stakeholdership, what sort of a posteriori stake would this performance grant them based on their state-sanctioned role of national 'carnival entertainers'? Here, it could be argued that this post-colonial carnivalesque visibility created a liminal third space where they were at once 'seen' and unseen, as what was being presented merely became a state-endorsed spectacle of cultural representation rather than anything that could be regarded as an authentic rendering of the diversities and complexities of contemporary post-colonial cultures and heritages. Ironically, it could be further argued that this performative liminal process of "Black" homogenising, at the expense of equally important inter-ethnic and religious identities, stored up challenges for the next decade in two ways. Firstly, in terms of the rise of disenfranchised Muslim communities (i.e., neglected religious and ethnic identities, stoked by perceptions of anti-Muslim foreign policy) and secondly, in terms of majoritarian Islamophobia (initially sparked by the perception of civic overspend on 'ethnic carnivalesque spectacles' at the expense of the majority).

## The 'Malign' Institution

In a report about police practice, written in response to the 1981 Brixton riots, Lord Scarman [125] admitted that, "racialism and discrimination against black people" was "often hidden, sometimes unconscious" (para. 6.35, p. 110). In amongst the widespread practice of 3S multiculturalism of this era, this marked an important conceptual move away from the 'fixed', individual and temporal notion of racism, as expressed by Powell. Scarman began to identify a less fixed, less overt and more malleable concept of racism. Moreover, this was one of the first times that *possible* institutional complicity in racism was identified[77] [126, 127], when he wrote that this type of "hidden" discrimination was most keenly felt in housing, education and employment. Even though the full implications of this report were not to be completely understood at the time, it did perhaps point to the inadequacies of 3S

[77] The 1981 Rampton and the 1985 Swann reports also concluded similar institutional complicity in racial discrimination but in the area of Education.

multiculturalism because this particular process of citizenisation was clearly failing to improve the social and economic conditions (housing, education and employment) of "black people" (p. 110). In terms of the police force (the focus of his report), Scarman did not go quite as far to identify a malign institution but he did concede that individuals within the institution could have had a malign effect on its overall management.

Eighteen years later, the "hidden," un-neutral, 'juridical' and 'discipline' powers of the institution were finally acknowledged by William MacPherson's [128] landmark report that was written as part of the Stephen Lawrence Enquiry.[78] [129]. In the report, for the first time we see a complete departure from the 'individualised' and 'fleeting' notions of racism and an arrival at a *structural*, endemic and *chronic* recognition of the possibility of a malign institution:

> 6.4 Racism in general terms consists of conduct or words or practices which disadvantage or advantage people because of their colour, culture, or ethnic origin. In its more subtle form it is as damaging as in its overt form.
>
> 6.5 We have been concerned with the more subtle and much discussed concept of racism referred to as institutional racism which (in the words of Dr. Robin Oakley) can influence police service delivery *"not solely through the deliberate actions of a small number of bigoted individuals, but through a more systematic tendency that could unconsciously influence police performance generally."* (p. 41) (original italics).

In his report, MacPherson explicitly builds on Scarman's notion of racism that was "hidden and sometimes unconscious." However, he deliberately contradicts Scarman's "rotten apple" [130] (para. 6.14) thesis to explain individual and aberrant racism in the police force:

> 6.48 There must be an unequivocal acceptance of the problem of institutional racism and its nature before it can be addressed, as it needs to be, in full partnership with members of minority ethnic communities. (p. 52)

[78] This was an enquiry into the 1993 racist fatal stabbing of the London black teenager, Stephen Lawrence. This became a landmark case because it highlighted serious structural weaknesses in the Metropolitan Police Force (Met) that allowed the six assailants to avoid prosecution. The ramifications of this case are still being felt today, as the Met is currently facing fresh allegations of police corruption in the handling of the case.

The importance of this acknowledgement cannot be underestimated because the term, "institutional racism" marked a paradigm shift in the public perception of our institutions where for the first time, our institutions (starting with the Police Forces) could actually be found to be malign, as they were shown to be capable of (re)producing structural inequalities. This report was all the more startling because addressing institutional racism, "in partnership with members of minority ethnic communities" would have constituted a political form of multiculturalism that would have adhered to Will Kymlicka's [131] third ideological principle; namely, states should acknowledge historical injustices done to its minorities. MacPherson's suggested act of introspection would have paved the way for a genuine national debate about ethnic minority *a priori stakeholdership* within the UK because the historical constitution and powers of our institutions[79] and how they produce and sustain, "institutional racism" would eventually needed to have been examined within the context of Britain's Post-Colonial history!

However, the immediate ramifications of MacPherson's revelatory recommendations were in the area of education. He suggests, "that consideration be given to amendment of the National Curriculum aimed at valuing cultural diversity and preventing racism, in order better to reflect the needs of a diverse society." (Chapter 47, para. 67) MacPherson also suggested that OFSTED should inspect the results of these amendments. These two recommendations could be considered as ushering in the next process of citizenisation, "Community Cohesion" [132].[80]

## Community Cohesion

With the US and London terrorist attacks in 2001 and 2005 respectively and the unrelated Oldham, Harehills and Bradford riots in the North of England in 2001 involving the perception of Muslim ill-treatment, the idea of a multiculturalism that promoted division (perhaps tacitly regarded as an over-celebration of diversity that led to self-imposed segregation) became a popular idea. This was summed up by the, "feelings of public outrage and disbelief that young British Muslims could feel so alienated from mainstream society that they could engage in acts of terrorism against their fellow citizens" [133]

[79] Starting with the Police Forces, all of our interconnected institutions would have needed the same scrutiny.

[80] More specifically the 2006 Community Cohesion act that put a statutory obligation on schools to promote community cohesion.

(p. 36). So ideas around race, ethnicity and religion became subsumed into a concept of "community" where there was "a veritable return to assimilationist ideals through the construction of need for greater integration and social solidarity" [134]. (p. 15) Indeed, community cohesion is not generally defined by its heterogeneity but by its homogeneity of values and "community." However, this new type of assimilation can also be viewed as a form of, "neo-racism" [135] where although the language of race had been replaced by the language of culture and values, structural racial discrimination continued unabated. This hegemony of dichotomous community "values" whose genesis lies in being, "either with us or against us" is only made possible because, as a nation, we decided to row back from defining a priori stakeholdership for our post-colonial communities as per the implications of MacPherson's findings. I will come back to this point, shortly.

## Equality and Diversity, the New 3S Multiculturalism?

The "institutional racism" that was so clearly identified a decade and a half earlier has now (currently) been morphed into the need to track 'equality' and 'diversity'. Equality and diversity within institutions have become the new 3S form of multiculturalism because structural barriers of discrimination are still not being systemically challenged[81] [136], which means that a priori stakeholdership continues to be left unaddressed. Instead, the structural barriers are subjected to, "crisis management" [137] (p. 37) initiatives for the sake of institutional 'representation' and symbolism. So, even though we have not quite returned to the literal ethnic carnivalesque of the 80's and 90's, we are currently reproducing it through our obsession with managerialism[82]

[81] Interestingly, in terms of sexual discrimination (leading to harassment and rape) in the armed forces, former Brigadier Nicky Moffat acknowledged that there were excellent senior male officers, who understood the issues and articulated the right message as regards equality and diversity. However, in terms of the lack of cultural change within the institution, she said that, "there are some who overly rely on equality and diversity statements…words on a page and they think that's the job done.."

[82] Looking back with 'nostalgia' to the then new wave of 80's managerialism where a colour-blind discourse on individualisation, standards and management was developed. Although nowadays ethnicity is certainly not colour-blind, its subsumption into the cloud of 'equality and diversity' is reminiscent of the new wave managerialism characterised by Louise Archer & Becky Francis as New Public Management (NPM). Of NPM's potential for deprioritising race, Barry Troyna observes that in education, "policymakers who had framed their policies along these lines had deliberately eschewed overt reference to racial descriptions, evaluations and prescriptions in preference to apparently more legitimate educational imperatives" (p. 309)

[138, 139], where 'spectacle' has been replaced by 'data' to represent institutional ethnic (and others') participation (or lack thereof). So whilst structural issues around ethnic representation are being subsumed and categorised into new Foucauldian neo-liberal knowledges and managed by new functionaries of the institutions, the 'carnival of data' has managed to shift the attention away from institutional reform back onto ethnic 'representation' and the ethnic communities themselves (as well as other marginalised communities); a process of statistical fetishsisation.

## 'Malign' Institutions (per)forming a 'Protective' State

Moreover, it would seem that in order to further distract from their 'malign' potential and to avoid real structural change, institutions appear to be modelling themselves on the (western) international cultural memory or call for *humanitarian* unity.[83] Institutions have been transformed not into composite images of transnational monism i.e., 'Empire' or 'Civilisation' but into composite images of a national protective *state*. Community cohesion as a concept born out of an international fear of terror is our current process of citizenisation (political multiculturalism), which we call the PREVENT strategy[84] [140]. PREVENT is rigorously policed and targets deemed 'at risk' are thoroughly pathologised[85] [141] in order to ensure cohesion (minimisation of threat levels). Here, we have a sleight of hand, where civic unity has now been deliberately conflated with (inter)national security. This is important because the perception of the need to prioritise national security[86] above

---

[83] Which in the UK manifests itself in its political form of multiculturalism (community cohesion) represented by the CONTEST programme.

[84] Part of the overall CONTEST anti-terrorism programme consisting of PURSUE: stopping terrorists from committing acts of terrorism, PREVENT: stopping people from becoming terrorists, PROTECT: strengthening (intelligence and infrastructural) protection against terrorism and PREPARE: strengthening our coping mechanisms in the event of a terrorist attack.

[85] Via the 'Channel Process', which aims to provide support to individuals at risk of being drawn into violent extremism. It draws on existing collaboration between local authorities, the police, statutory partners (such as the education sector, social services, children's and youth services and offender management services) and the local community and has three objectives: to identify individuals at risk of being drawn into violent extremism; to assess the nature and extent of that risk; to develop the most appropriate support for the individuals concerned.

[86] This perception is crucial because Charlotte Heath-Kelly reminds us that our present form of citizenisation is built on managing risk factors, which means having to manage the unknown or as Heath-Kelly calls it, "opacity". She goes on to suggest that communities that

everything is what is giving the state the potential powers to curb not just civic rights but human rights too.

Dan Hyde [142] writes about how the Draft Communications Bill is at risk of endangering our internet data protection/privacy by, "allowing the security services to monitor people's emails, internet browsing, phone calls and text messages." Jon Snow [143] examines the implications of the Conservative administration's plans to repeal the 1998 Human Rights Act that ties the UK into the 1953 European Convention on Human Rights (ECHR). This repeal has an eerie resemblance to the ideological call for civic unity around British values that are as yet unexplained because the Conservatives would like to replace the Human Rights Act with an equally as of yet unspecified British Bill of Rights. Ironically, the vagueness of this ambition to repeal the Human Rights Act actually threatens to dismantle the devolution of the three Kingdoms (Northern Ireland, Scotland and Wales) because their devolved powers were granted on the express understanding of the incorporation of the ECHR via the Human Rights Act in all of their devolution settlements. This also included the Good Friday Agreement for Northern Ireland.

## CONCLUSION

Our form of Community Cohesion (currently the CONTEST programme) has allowed the state through its institutions to progressively erode both our human *and* civic rights. It is doing this to the point where *everyone* is now at risk of being dehumanised and treated as mere agents of state function; namely, homogenous *agents* of national security rather than autonomous heterogeneous *human beings*.

The performative nature of UK political multiculturalism through its various processes of citizenisation has meant that its stubborn ideological reluctance to acknowledge a priori stakeholdership for its post-colonial minorities has shown it to be little more than a political tool of Foucauldian population control rather than a genuine mechanism for equality and civic

are deemed to be 'opaque' are put under greater surveillance than others whilst no effort is made to understand them (or their stake). Rather profoundly, risk becomes performative as it is generated by perceived opacity and its greater need for surveillance. So this political process of citizenisation hails the process of dehumanisation into being which in turn generates further alienation for which the communities are themselves blamed. Therefore, with the need to gain ever more control over (perceived) opacity, everyone's human and civic rights have become endangered.

acceptance. As discussed throughout this chapter, multiculturalism's ideological inability to address structural inequalities (a priori stakeholdership within the national cultural memory) at national and local levels has left it at the mercy of international geopolitical agendas that threaten everyone's civic and human liberties (rights). However, this is even a profound threat to the UK's own historical sub-national multicultural identity and cultural memories.

## REFERENCES

[1] Finney, N., & Simpson, L. (2009). Population Dynamics: The Roles of Natural Change and Migration in Producing the Ethnic Mosaic. *Journal of Ethnic and Migration Studies, 35*(9), 1479-1496.

[2] Mirza, H. S. (2005). The more things change, the more they stay the same: assessing Black underachievement 35 years on. In B. Richardson (Ed.), *Tell it like it is: How our schools fail Black children* (pp. 111-118). London: Bookmarks Publication.

[3] Gilroy, P. (2005). Multiculture, double consciousness and the 'war on terror'. *Patterns of Prejudice, 39*(4), 431-443.

[4] Butler, J. (1997). *The Psychic Life of Power.* Stanford: Stanford University Press.

[5] Du Bois, W. (1935 [1998]). *Black Reconstruction in America 1860-1880.* New York: The Free Press.

[6] Becker, B. (2015, May 24). *The revolutionary origins of Memorial Day and its political hijacking.* Retrieved May 25, 2015, from Liberation. http://www.liberationnews.org/revolutionary-origins-memorial-day-political-hijacking/

[7] Clennon, O. (2015). *Urban Dialectics, The Market and Youth Engagement: The 'Black' Face of Eurocentrism.* New York: Nova Science Publishers.

[8] Nora, P. (1996). General Introduction: Between Memory and History. In L. D. Krtizmann (Ed.), *Realms of Memory: Rethinking the French Past, Vol1: Conflict and Divisions* (A. Goldhammer, Trans., pp. 1-20). New York: Columbia University Press.

[9] Nyong'o, T. (2012). Queer Africa and the Fantasy of Virtual Participation. *WSQ: Women's Studies Quarterly, 40*(1-2), 40-63.

[10] Meer, N., & Modood, T. (2012). How does Interculturalism Contrast with Multiculturalism? *Journal of Intercultural Studies, 33*(2), 175 - 196.

[11] Vertovec, S., & Wessendorf, S. (Eds.). (2010). *The Multiculturalism Backlash: Eurpoean discourses, policies and practices.* Abingdon and New York: Routledge.

[12] Meer, N., & Modood, T. (2012). How does Interculturalism Contrast with Multiculturalism? *Journal of Intercultural Studies, 33*(2), 175 - 196.

[13] CMEB (Commission on the Future of Multi-Ethnic Britain). (2000). *The Future of multi-ethnic Britain.* London: Profile Books.

[14] Byrne, B. (2014). *Making Citizens.* Basingstoke: Palgrave Politics of Identity and Citizenship.

[15] Assmann, J., & Czaplicka, J. (1995). Collective Memory and Cultural Identity. *New German Critique, 65*(Spring - Summer), 125-133.

[16] Smith, A. D. (1998). *Nationalism and modernism: a critical survey of recent theories of naitons and nationalism.* London: Routledge.

[17] Kymlicka, W. (1995). *Multicultural citizenship.* Oxford: Oxford University Press.

[18] Du Bois, W. (1935 [1998]). *Black Reconstruction in America 1860-1880.* New York: The Free Press.

[19] Jones, G. (2005, August 3). *Multicultural Britain is not working, says Tory chief.* Retrieved July 17, 2015, from The Telegraph: http://www.telegraph.co.uk/news/uknews/1495397/Multicultural-Britain-is-not-working-says-Tory-chief.html

[20] Weale, S. (2015, March 30). *Teachers urged to 'disengage' from promotion of British values.* Retrieved March 31, 2015, from The Guardian: http://www.theguardian.com/politics/2015/mar/30/teachers-urged-to-disengage-from-promotion-of-british-values

[21] Parekh, B. (2000). *Rethinking Multiculturalism: Cultural Diversity and Political Theory.* London: Macmillan Press Ltd.

[22] Sugar Media and Marketing Limited. (2015, April 10). *Black History Month 2015.* Retrieved April 10, 2015, from Black History Month: http://www.blackhistorymonth.org.uk/

[23] Kirkup, J. (2015, February 13). *British Muslims: integration and segregation are about economics, not values.* Retrieved May 13, 2015, from The Telegraph: http://www.telegraph.co.uk/news/uknews/immigration/11409181/British-Muslims-integration-and-segregation-are-about-economics-not-values.html

[24] Clennon, O. (Ed.). (2014). *Alternative Education and Community Engagement: Making Education a Priority.* Basingstoke: Palgrave Macmillan.

[25] Chalabi, M. (2014, January 8). *Rising unemployment for UK's ethnic minorities: who's affected?* Retrieved April 9, 2015, from The Guardian: http://www.theguardian.com/news/datablog/2014/jan/08/rising-unemployment-for-uk-ethnic-minorities-race-whos-affected

[26] Phillips, D. (2006). Parallel lives? Challenging discourses of British Muslim self-segregation. *Environment and Planning D: Society and Space, 24*(1), 25 – 40.

[27] Alexander, C. (2002). Beyond Black: Re-Thinking the Colour/Culture Divide. *Ethnic and Racial Studies, 25*(4), 552-571.

[28] NARA. (2015, April 2). *The Charters of Freedom: The Declaration of Independence.* Retrieved April 2, 2015, from The U.S. National Archives and Records Administration: http://www.archives.gov/exhibits/charters/declaration_transcript.html

[29] Olusoga, D. (2015, July 12). *The history of British slave ownership has been buried: now its scale can be revealed.* Retrieved July 12, 205, from The Guardian: http://www.theguardian.com/world/2015/jul/12/british-history-slavery-buried-scale-revealed?CMP=share_btn_tw

[30] Long, E. (1774). *The History of Jamaica* (Vol. 2). London: T. Lowndes.

[31] Du Bois, W. (1935 [1998]). *Black Reconstruction in America 1860-1880.* New York: The Free Press.

[32] Bundles, A. (2015, August 15). *Race in the US: Know your history.* Retrieved August 15, 2015, from Al Jazeera: http://www.aljazeera.com/indepth/features/2015/08/race-history-ferguson-150814082921736.html

[33] Baudrillard, J. (1981). *Simulacra and Simulation.* Michigan: University Michigan Press.

[34] Acemoglu, D., Johnson, S., & Robinson, J. A. (2001). The Colonial Origins of Comparative Development: An Empirical Investigation. *American Economic Review, 91*(Dec 5th), 1369 - 1401.

[35] Bourdieu, P. (1984). *Distinction: A Social Critique of the Judgement of Taste.* (R. Nice, Trans.) Cambridge, MA: Harvard University Press.

[36] Benjamin, W. (1999). *The Arcades Project.* (R. Tiedemann, Ed., H. Eiland, & K. McLaughlin, Trans.) Cambridge MA: Harvard University Press.

[37] Bhabha, H. K. (1994). *The Location of Culture.* London, New York: Routledge.

[38] Fanon, F. (1963[1961]). *The Wretched of the Earth.* (C. Farrington, Trans.) New York: Grove Press.

[39] Butler, J. (1997). *The Psychic Life of Power.* Stanford: Stanford University Press.

[40] Carter, M. (2014, January 23). *British readers and writers need to embrace their colonial past.* Retrieved April 22, 2015, from The Guardian: http://www.theguardian.com/books/2014/jan/23/british-readers-writers-embrace-colonial-past

[41] Scott, P. (1966). *The Jewel in the Crown.* London: Heinemann.

[42] Rutland, P. (Writer), Moore, D., & Tucker, A. (Directors). (2015). *Indian Summers* [TV Drama].

[43] Clarke, S. (2004). *Jonathan Strange and Mr Norrell.* London: Bloomsbury.

[44] Asante, A. (Director). (2014). *Belle* [Motion Picture].

[45] Parekh, B. (2000). *Rethinking Multiculturalism: Cultural Diversity and Political Theory.* London: Macmillan Press Ltd.

[46] Renan, E. (1996[1882]). What is Nation? In G. Eley, & R. G. Suny (Eds.), *Becoming National: A Reader* (pp. 41 - 55). New York and Oxford: Oxford University Press.

[47] Miller, D. (1995). *On Nationality.* Oxford: Clarendon Press.

[48] Miller, D. (1976). *Social Justice.* Oxford: Clarendon Press.

[49] Byrne, B. (2014). *Making Citizens.* Basingstoke: Palgrave Politics of Identity and Citizenship.

[50] Vertovec, S. (2007). Super-diversity and its implications. *Ethnic and Racial Studies,* 30(6), 1024-1054

[51] Huntington, S. P. (1998). *The Clash of Civilizations and the Remaking of World Order.* New York: Simon and Schuster.

[52] Huntington, S. P. (1993). The Clash of Civilizations. *Foreign Affairs, 72*(3), 22-49.

[53] Weber, C. (2005). *International Relations Theory: A critical introduction* (Second ed.). Abingdon and New York: Routledge.

[54] CNN.com. (2001, November 6). *War against Terror.* Retrieved April 22, 2015, from CNN.com/US: http://edition.cnn.com/2001/US/11/06/ret.bush.coalition/index.html

[55] Gilroy, P. (2010). *Darker than Blue: On the Moral Economies of Black Atlantic Culture.* Cambridge, MA: The Belknap Press of Harvard University Press.

[56] Anderson, C. E. (2003). *Eyes Off the Prize: The United Nations and the African American Struggle for Human Rights, 1944 - 1955.* Cambridge (UK): Cambridge University Press.

[57] ourdocuments.gov. (2015, April 27). *15th Amendment to the U.S. Constitution: Voting Rights (1870).* Retrieved April 27, 2015, from 100

Milestone Documents: http://www.ourdocuments.gov/doc.php?flash=true&doc=44

[58] Clennon, O. (2013). A commentary: Did multiculturalism really win the race to the Whitehouse? *International Journal of Media & Cultural Politics, 9*(3), 297–304.

[59] Malcolm X. (1970). Malcolm X's Speech at the Founding Rally of the Organization of Afro-American Unity. In Malcolm X, *By Any Means* (pp. 35 - 67). New York: Pathfinder Press.

[60] Luther King, M. (1963, August 28). *I have a dream speech*. Retrieved April 22, 2015, from American History: From Revolution to Reconstruction and beyond: http://www.let.rug.nl/usa/documents/1951-/martin-luther-kings-i-have-a-dream-speech-august-28-1963.php

[61] Hassan, R. (1995). Are Human Rights Compatible with Islam? The Issue of the Rights of Women in Muslim Communities. In D. C. Maguire (Ed.), *Human Rights in China and Islam* (pp. 25 - 38). Washington, D.C.: The Religious Consultation on Population, Reproductive Health and Ethics.

[62] Kymlicka, W. (2010). The rise and fall of multiculturalism? New debates on inclusion and accommodation in diverse societies. *International Social Science Journal, 61*(199), 97-112.

[63] Renteln, A. D. (2013). *International Human Rights: Universalism Versus Relativism.* New Orleans: Quid Pro Books.

[64] Kegley, C. W. (1993). The Neoidealist Moment in International Studies? Realist Myths and the New International Realities. *International Studies Quarterly, 37*(2), 131-146.

[65] Kegley, C. W. (1995). The neoliberal challenge to realist theories of world politics: an introduction. In C. W. Kegley (Ed.), *Controversies in International Relations Theory: Realism and the Neoliberal Challenge* (pp. 1 - 24). New York: St. Martin's Press.

[66] Waltz, K. N. (1959). *Man, the state and war: a theoretical analysis.* New York: Columbia University Press.

[67] Smith, S. (2000). The discipline of international relations: still an American social science? *British Journal of Politics and International Relations, 2*(3), 374–402.

[68] Hardt, M., & Negri, A. (2009). *Empire.* Cambridge, M.A.: Harvard University Press.

[69] Said, E. (1978). *Orientalism.* New York: Vintage Books.

[70] Lorenz, J. (2003). *The Coalition of the Willing.* Stanford, C.A.: Stanford University. Available at http://web.stanford.edu/class/e297a/The%20 Coalition%20of%20the%20Willing.htm.

[71] Uludag, M., & Molyneux, J. (2014). Racism and Islamophobia. *Irish Marxist Review, 3*(10), 64-69.

[72] Vertigans, S. (2010). British Muslims and the UK government's 'war on terror' within: evidence of a clash of civilizations or emergent de-civilizing processes? *The British Journal of Sociology, 61*(1), 26-44.

[73] Saeed, A. (2007). Media, racism and Islamophobia: the representation of Islam and Muslims in the media. *Sociology Compass, 1*(2), 443 - 462.

[74] Jaspal, R., & Cinnirella, M. (2010). Media representations of British Muslims and hybridized threats to identity. *Contemporary Islam: Dynamics of Muslim Life, 4*(3), 289 - 310.

[75] Hasan, M. (2015, July 5). *Life for British Muslims since 7/7 – abuse, suspicion and constant apologies.* Retrieved July 7, 2015, from The Guardian: http://www.theguardian.com/commentisfree/2015/jul/05/ british-muslims-7-july-london-bombings

[76] Heath-Kelly, C. (2013). Counter-Terrorism and the Counterfactual: Producing the 'Radicalisation' Discourse and the UK PREVENT Strategy. *The British Journal of Politics & International Relations, 15*(3), 394–415.

[77] Horgan, J., & Taylor, M. (2011). Disengagement, De-radicalization and the Arc of Terrorism: Future Directions for Research. In R. Coolsaet (Ed.), *'Jihadi Terrorism and the Radicalisation Challenge: European and American Experiences* (pp. 173-186). Farnham: Ashgate.

[78] Jacobs, B. D. (1986). *Black Politics and Urban Crisis in Britain.* Cambridge (UK): Cambridge University Press.

[79] Travis, A. (2014, April 30). *Stop and Search: Theresa May announces reform of police stop-and-search powers.* Retrieved May 3, 2015, from The Guardian: http://www.theguardian.com/law/2014/apr/30/theresa-may-reform-police-stop-and-search-powers

[80] Goodman, A., & Ruggiero, V. (2008). Crime, Punishment, and Ethnic Minorities in England and Wales. *Race/Ethnicity: Multidisciplinary Global Contexts, 2*(1), 53-68.

[81] Modood, T., & May, S. (2001). Multiculturalism and education in Britain: an internally contested debate. *International Journal of Educational Research, 35*, 305–317.

[82] Bourdieu, P. (1984). *Distinction: A Social Critique of the Judgement of Taste.* (R. Nice, Trans.) Cambridge, MA: Harvard University Press.

[83] Foucault, M. (1978). *The History of Sexuality Volume 1: An Introduction.* (R. Hurley, Trans.) New York: Pantheon Books.

[84] European Commission. (2015, May 4). *Free Movement - EU nationals.* Retrieved May 4, 2015, from Employment, Social Affairs and Inclusion: http://ec.europa.eu/social/main.jsp?catId=457

[85] Holmwood, J., & Bhambra, G. K. (2015, July 3). *Capitalist dispossession and new justifications of slavery.* Retrieved 4 July, 2015, from openDemocracy: https://www.opendemocracy.net/beyondslavery/john-holmwood-gurminder-k-bhambra/capitalist-dispossession-and-new-justifications-of-s

[86] Posner, E. A., & Weyl, G. (2014, November 6). *A Radical Solution to Global Income Inequality: Make the U.S. More Like Qatar.* Retrieved July 4, 2015, from New Republic: http://www.newrepublic.com/article/120179/how-reduce-global-income-inequality-open-immigration-policies

[87] Brooks-Higginbotham, E. (1993). *Righteous Discontent: The Women's Movement in the Black Baptist Church 1880 - 1920.* Cambridge, MA: Harvard University Press.

[88] Washington, B. T. (Ed.). (1903). *The Negro problem; a series of articles by representative American Negroes of today.* New York: J. Pott & Company.

[89] King, L. (2013). The Relevance and Redefining of Du Bois's Talented Tenth: Two Centuries Later. *Papers and Publications: Interdisciplinary Journal of Undergraduate Research, 2*(1), Article 9.

[90] Emmons, W. R., & Noeth, B. J. (2015, Issue 12). *Why Didn't Higher Education Protect Hispanic and Black Wealth?* Retrieved August 19, 2015, from Federal Reserve Bank of St Louis: https://www.stlouisfed.org/publications/in-the-balance/issue12-2015/why-didnt-higher-education-protect-hispanic-and-black-wealth

[91] Wells-Barnett, I. B. (2014[1892]). *On Lynchings.* New York: Dover Publications.

[92] Ogbu, J. U. (2004). Collective Identity and the Burden of "Acting White" in Black History, Community and Education. *Urban Review, 36*(1), 1-35.

[93] Clennon, O. (Ed.). (2014). *Alternative Education and Community Engagement: Making Education a Priority.* Basingstoke: Palgrave Macmillan.

[94] Smith, M. D. (2013, September 16). *Respectability Politics Won't Save Us: On the Death of Jonathan Ferrell.* Retrieved April 5, 2015, from

The Nation: http://m.thenation.com/blog/176183-respectability-politics-wont-save-us-death-jonathan-ferrell

[95] Gross, K. N. (1997). Examining the Politics of Respectability in African American Studies. *Almanac, 43*(28), http://www.upenn.edu/almanac/v43/n28/benchmrk.html.

[96] Johnson, E. P., & Henderson, M. G. (Eds.). (2005). *Black Queer Studies: A Critical Anthology.* Durham, NC: Duke University Press.

[97] McKesson, D. (2015, August 9). *Ferguson and beyond: how a new civil rights movement began – and won't end.* Retrieved August 9, 2015, from The Guardian: http://www.theguardian.com/commentisfree/2015/aug/09/ferguson-civil-rights-movement-deray-mckesson-protest?CMP=twt_gu

[98] Scott, S. (2013, July 25). *PC Blakelock: black people are waiting for justice too.* Retrieved August 15, 2015, from The Guardian: http://www.theguardian.com/commentisfree/2013/jul/25/blakelock-black-people-justice-tottenham-police

[99] Jacobs, B. D. (1986). *Black Politics and Urban Crisis in Britain.* Cambridge (UK): Cambridge University Press.

[100] Mirza, H. S. (2010). *Multicultural Education in England.* London: International Alliance of Leading Education Institutes (IALEI), Institute of Education, University of London.

[101] Powell, E. (2007 [1968], November 6). *The Rivers of Blood Speech.* Retrieved July 23, 2013, from The Telegraph: http://www.telegraph.co.uk/comment/3643823/Enoch-Powells-Rivers-of-Blood-speech.html

[102] Virgil. (2015, May 7). *Aeneid VI.* Retrieved May 7, 2015, from Poetry in Translation:http://www.poetryintranslation.com/PITBR/Latin/VirgilAeneidVI.htm#anchor_Toc2242923

[103] Mirza, H. S. (2010). *Multicultural Education in England.* London: International Alliance of Leading Education Institutes (IALEI), Institute of Education, University of London.

[104] Gillborn, D. (2005). Education Policy as an Act White Supremacy: Whiteness, Critical Race Theory and Education Reform. *Journal of Education Policy, 20*(4), 485-505.

[105] Delgado, R., & Stefancic, J. (2001). *Critical Race Theory: An Introduction.* New York: New York University Press.

[106] Taylor, E. (2009). The Foundations of Critical Race Theory in Education: An Introduction. In E. Taylor, D. Gillborn, & G. Ladson-Billings (Eds.), *Foundations of Critical Race Theory In Education* (pp. 1-13). New York: Routledge.

[107] Mirza, H. S. (2009). *Race Gender and Educational Desire: Why Black Women Succeed and Fail.* London: Routledge.

[108] Mirza, H. S. (2010). *Multicultural Education in England.* London: International Alliance of Leading Education Institutes (IALEI), Institute of Education, University of London.

[109] Gillborn, D. (2004). Anti-racism: from policy to praxis. In G. Ladson-Billings, & D. Gillborn (Eds.), *The RoutledgeFalmer Reader in Multicultural Education* (pp. 35-48). London: RoutledgeFalmer.

[110] Burke, J. C. (2008). Milestones: 'Like the Roman'. Enoch Powell and English Immigration Law. *Amsterdam Law Forum, 1*(1), 131 - 138.

[111] Pidd, H. (2015, August 11). *Bradford stabbing prompts UK Asians to warn of racism towards black people.* Retrieved August 28, 2015, from The Guardian: http://www.theguardian.com/world/2015/aug/11/bradford-stabbing-prompts-uk-asians-to-warn-of-racism-towards-black-people

[112] Heath-Kelly, C. (2013). Counter-Terrorism and the Counterfactual: Producing the 'Radicalisation' Discourse and the UK PREVENT Strategy. *The British Journal of Politics & International Relations, 15*(3), 394–415.

[113] Tomlinson, S. (2008). *Race and Education: Policy and Politics in Britain.* Berkshire: Open University Press.

[114] Socialist Worker. (2002, May 4). *Thatcher echo from Blunkett boosts Nazis.* Retrieved September 2, 2013, from Socialist Worker: http://www.socialistworker.co.uk/art/5598/Thatcher+echo+from+Blunkett+boosts+Nazis

[115] Troyna, B. (1992). Can you see the join? An historical analysis of multicultural and antiracist education policies. In D. Gill, B. M. Mayor, & M. Blair (Eds.), *Racism and education; structures and strategies* (pp. 63-91). London: Sage.

[116] Cities of Migration. (2012, May 31). *The World in a City: The Olympic Diversity and Inclusion Strategy.* Retrieved April 3, 2015, from Cities of Migration: http://citiesofmigration.ca/good_idea/the-world-in-a-city-the-olympic-diversity-and-inclusion-strategy/

[117] Vertovec, S. (2007). Super-diversity and its implications. *Ethnic and Racial Studies,* 30(6), 1024-1054

[118] Clennon, O. (2015). *Urban Dialectics, The Market and Youth Engagement: The 'Black' Face of Eurocentrism.* New York: Nova Science Publishers.

[119] Krishnaswarmy, R. (2002). The criticism of culture and the culture of criticism at the intersection of postcolonialism and globalisation theory. *Diacritics, 32*(2), 106 - 126.

[120] CMEB (Commission on the Future of Multi-Ethnic Britain). (2000). *The Future of multi-ethnic Britain.* London: Profile Books.

[121] Alibhai-Brown, Y. (2000). *After multiculturalism.* London: Foreign Policy Centre.

[122] Vertovec, S. (2007). Super-diversity and its implications. *Ethnic and Racial Studies,* 30(6), 1024-1054

[123] Vertovec, S. (2007). Super-diversity and its implications. *Ethnic and Racial Studies,* 30(6), 1024-1054

[124] Gillborn, D. (2004). Anti-racism: from policy to praxis. In G. Ladson-Billings, & D. Gillborn (Eds.), *The RoutledgeFalmer Reader in Multicultural Education* (pp. 35-48). London: RoutledgeFalmer.

[125] Scarman. (1981). *The Scarman Report.* London: HMSO. pp. 204-206 also available at http://www.univ-paris13.fr/ANGLICISTES/POIRIER/IUFM/TextesIUFM/1981Scarman.pdf.

[126] Rampton. (1981). *The Rampton Report: West Indian Children in our Schools.* Retrieved September 2, 2013, from Education in England: http://www.educationengland.org.uk/documents/rampton/rampton1981.html

[127] Swann. (1985). *The Swann Report: Education for All.* Retrieved September 2, 2013, from Education in England: http://www.educationengland.org.uk/documents/swann/

[128] MacPherson. (1999, February). *The MacPherson report.* Retrieved September 2, 2013, from Büro zur Umsetzung von Gleichbehandlung: http://www.archive.official-documents.co.uk/document/cm42/4262/4262.htm

[129] Press Association. (2014, November 24). *Stephen Lawrence murder: insufficient evidence to prosecute sixth suspect*. Retrieved April 13, 2015, from The Guardian: http://www.theguardian.com/uk-news/2014/nov/24/stephen-lawrence-murder-insufficient-evidence-sixth-suspect

[130] MacPherson. (1999, February). *The MacPherson report.* Retrieved September 2, 2013, from Büro zur Umsetzung von Gleichbehandlung: http://www.archive.official-documents.co.uk/document/cm42/4262/4262.htm

[131] Kymlicka, W. (1995). *Multicultural citizenship.* Oxford: Oxford University Press.

[132] GOV.UK. (2011, February 28). *FOI Release: Community Cohesion.* Retrieved August 28, 2013, from Department for Education: https://www.gov.uk/government/publications/community-cohesion/community-cohesion#contents

[133] Cremin, H., & Warwick, P. (2008). Multiculturalism is Dead: long live community cohesion? A Case Study of an Educational Methodology to Empower Young People as Global Citizens. *Research in Comparative and International Education, 3*(1), 36-49.

[134] Mirza, H. S. (2010). *Multicultural Education in England.* London: International Alliance of Leading Education Institutes (IALEI), Institute of Education, University of London.

[135] Balibar, E. (1991). Is there a "neo-racism"? In E. Balibar, & I. Wallerstein (Eds.), *Race, Nation, Class: Ambiguous Identities* (pp. 17-28). New York: Verso.

[136] Kotecha, S. (2015, May 19). *Army must 'speak out' against harassment, says brigadier.* Retrieved May 25, 2015, from BBC News: http://www.bbc.co.uk/news/uk-32780009

[137] Rowe, M. (Ed.). (2013). *Policing beyond Macpherson: Issues in policing, race and society.* London: Willan Publishing.

[138] Archer, L., & Francis, B. (2007). *Understanding minority ethnic achievement: race, gender, class and 'success'.* London: Routledge.

[139] Troyna, B. (1987). Beyond Multiculturalism: towards the enactment of anti-racist education in policy, provision and pedagogy. *Oxford Review of Education, 13*(3), 307-320.

[140] Home Office. (2011). *CONTEST: The United Kingdom's Strategy for Countering Terrorism.* London: HM Government.

[141] Institute for Strategic Dialogue. (2014). *Channel Process.* Retrieved May 25, 2015, from Counterextremism.org: https://www.counter extremism.org/resources/details/id/115/channel-process

[142] Hyde, D. (2015, May 8). *Now Tories can push through 'snoopers' charter', says May.* Retrieved May 17, 2015, from The Telegraph: http://www.telegraph.co.uk/news/general-election-2015/11591937/Now-Tories-can-push-through-snoopers-charter-says-May.html

[143] Snow, J. (2015, May 15). *Can Gove push through plan to scrap human rights act?* Retrieved May 17, 2015, from Channel 4 News: http://www.channel4.com/news/human-rights-act-michael-gove-opposition-snp-david-davis

In: International Perspectives of Multiculturalism ISBN: 978-1-63483-971-6
Editor: Ornette D. Clennon 

*Chapter 3*

# HUMAN DIGNITY: DOUBLE DIMENSIONS THEORY

***Narciso Leandro Xavier Baez****
Universidade do Oeste de Santa Catarina, Brazil

## ABSTRACT

This chapter aims to present a new theory about human rights that offers objective tools to evaluate cases involving polemical situations regarding cultural traditions. Narciso Baez proposes a theoretical framework that allows us to evaluate whether a controversial practice represents a cultural expression of human dignity or instead, a violation of human rights. Baez's current proposal seeks to overcome the antagonisms between the universalism vs. cultural relativism debate.

**Keywords:** human rights, universalism, relativism, burka, human dignity

## INTRODUCTION

When basic human rights are discussed they are normally associated with the expression of high moral principles and political ideals relating to the

* Email: narciso.baez@gmail.com

protection and realisation of human dignity[1] [1] and the freedoms associated with it. However, the generality of the term combined with the difficulty of understanding what human dignity has come to mean, has created problems in understanding when a concrete fact is a moral practice adopted within a social group or when the same fact becomes a violation of a human right. The problem lies in the evaluation of each concrete case because the moral interpretations made by each culture often diverge and may even be contradictory.

To illustrate the issue, this study examines the situation of the use of the burka, a garment worn by women in some Muslim societies according to religious belief. The burka covers the entire body, including the face, and has a small piece of mesh at eye level that allows the user to see without being seen. To some Western cultures, the use of this garment characterises the degradation of women, which is why in countries like France it has been banned in public places. We observe how a moral practice in two different cultural contexts (one society requiring its use, the other forbidding it) is capable of generating antagonistic and seemingly irreconcilable responses, leading to reflection on the underlying issue: whether it is a real violation of fundamental human rights or simply a lifestyle choice based on the beliefs of a culture. The difficulty in responding to this question arises because there is still no clear understanding about which human rights are fundamental; there are many doubts about what characteristics a right must possess to be recognised as fundamental and to what extent rights should be universally observed or relativised according to the moral values adopted by each society. This theoretical gap hinders the resolution of practical issues such as the burka question and justifies the need for research on the epistemology of fundamental human rights as a way of understanding their limits and applications, ensuring that the process of identifying attributes that may or may not be recognised as fundamental rights is clear and objective.

This work aims to develop this discussion by studying the philosophical and legal aspects of fundamental human rights with the aim of identifying an objective way to evaluate individual cases and distinguish cultural practice from violations of human dignity. To this end, we will discuss the morphology of fundamental human rights and the ethical characteristics of the legal rights

[1] In this work, the term *human dignity* is used to provide[1] an abstract representation of an attribute given to humankind as a whole, thereby avoiding the use of the term *dignity of the human person*, which is associated with the attribute of an individual person. This is the same distinction made by Ingo Wolfgang Sarlet's *Dignidade da Pessoa Humana e Direitos Fundamentais na Constituição Federal de 1988.*

that make up this category. Based on this study, I will form an ethical concept of fundamental human rights, using the situation of the French government's controversial ban on wearing a veil, in order to demonstrate the usefulness of this definition for real cases.

## MORPHOLOGY OF FUNDAMENTAL HUMAN RIGHTS

At the outset of the analysis of the morphology of fundamental human rights, it must be noted that there is no semantic agreement in the field about the terminology and the conceptual range of fundamental rights.[2] Moreover, the term is commonly used to define the phenomenon of the assertion of human rights in the internal constitutional framework of states, which becomes confused with what most academic writers interpret as civil rights [2].

To establish the semantic agreement necessary for understanding the theoretical context proposed here, human rights must be understood as a genus that contains species: fundamental human rights and civil rights. Fundamental human rights constitute an essential standard for the implementation of human rights and are responsible for protecting the basic dimension of human dignity, which will be detailed below, while civil rights represent the affirmation of human rights at the internal state level.

But why separate the categories of human rights and fundamental human rights? The need for this distinction lies in the fact that human rights (as a genus) have been formed historically [3] according to different standards of influence. Currently, we talk about environmental human rights, economic human rights and cultural human rights, among others [4], which are implemented asymmetrically within the social, economic, political and cultural limits of each state. This asymmetrical development shows that this category is developing to varying degrees, ranging from the protection of basic human needs to the most sophisticated forms of cultural, economic and social dignity.

### Human Rights As a Genus

In order to understand fundamental human rights, fully, one must first study their origin, or rather, the genus of human rights. One can find numerous

[2] This term is often used synonymously with human rights, individual rights, public subjective rights, rights of man, fundamental freedoms and civil liberties.

proposals in the search for a definition of human rights, ranging from their association with natural law [5] to their use as a minimum standard [6] that serves to legitimise the legal systems of states and reduce pluralism among the people. The most widespread concept, however, is that human rights constitute a set of rights inherent to all human beings, who possess them simply because they belong to the human species [7]. Thus, these would be inherent moral rights [8] that must be recognised in individuals without distinction and regardless of personal covenants or rules of law [9]. There are also those who simplify the issue to assert that human rights are those contained within the Universal Declaration of Human Rights, promulgated by the United Nations in 1948 [10].

However, the proposals listed above do not offer a satisfactory explanation of how to recognise a particular right as integral to the human rights category. This is the case because these concepts are limited to show certain traits, without explaining why the rights therein should be considered human rights.

The search for an objective concept for this class of rights must begin with the Universal Declaration of Human Rights of the United Nations because it was the first instrument of human rights proclaimed by a global international organisation [11] and, for many researchers [12], represents a general consensus about the validity of a system of values founded on humanity. Note, however, that the issue in this analysis is not the process of asserting human rights. What is necessary to understand is why certain values were chosen to be included in the UN Declaration and what they possessed that was so important that they had become an object of concern and proclamation by an entire community of states in the international domain.

The understanding of the rights enshrined in the Universal Declaration requires the analysis of events that occurred in the years preceding its enactment. In the period between 1940 and 1945, World War II left humanity with the experience of the cruelty of the Nazi concentration camps and the destructive effect of nuclear weapons on Hiroshima and Nagasaki [13]. Facing the crisis created in the social, political and economic spheres at the end of this devastating period, nations understood the need to create an international force to maintain peace and respect for human life [14]. Thus, the development of a joint declaration on the rights of man was sought that would be capable of reconciling and inspiring respect for humanity and, at the same time, would be broad enough to be understood and adapted by the peoples of the world, taking into account their different cultures [15]. In 1947, during preparations for the drafting of this document, UNESCO sent a questionnaire with considerations and problems of both a general and specialised character to the writers and thinkers of different nations. The questionnaires were sent out to ascertain the moral and philosophical doctrines adopted by different groups and arguments, which could lend theoretical support to the set of rights to be included in the Declaration. The main issue to be resolved at that time was the following, "In today's world, what are the theoretical bases, the practical range and the effective guarantees of specific rights or freedoms such as the following..." [16] (pp. 14 – 15) It proceeded to list freedom of conscience, religion, speech, assembly, association, locomotion, living free from all fear, the equality of economic, social and educational opportunities, employment, access to subsistence and all other rights and freedoms [17]. Among the responses received were declarations from Mahatma Gandhi, Benedetto Croce, Aldous Huxley, Jacques Maritain, Teilhard de Chardin, John Lewis, Harold Laski and Salvador de Madariaga. UNESCO attempted to synthesise these responses and use them as a philosophical basis for the justification and rational interpretation of rights that would be contained in the Declaration of Human Rights [18].

However, when the questionnaire responses were returned, it became apparent that the issue was more complex than the UNESCO Commission for Philosophical Foundations of Human Rights could imagine. The declarations received, in addition to the positions taken by members of the Commission, showed the division of opinion between those who recognised human rights as natural rights [3] and those who saw human rights as a result of a variable and relative historical process, depending on the cultural context adopted by each society [19]. According to Jacques Maritain, the ambassador who headed the French delegation in this discussion, the difficulty experienced by the Commission at the time was this ideological rivalry. It was so irreconcilable that at times, there was agreement from all parties on the list of rights that should be recognised as human rights, but there was no consensus on why these rights should be recognised as belonging to this category [20]. These difficulties led Maritain to say that only when they could go beyond a mere enumeration of rights to key values that could be substantiated and that could achieve a practical criterion for use would they be able to ensure respect for this category [21].

Despite all the difficulties, the UNESCO Commission achieved consensus on at least one element that should be the basis and measure for all rights with a claim to be recognised as human rights. This element was incorporated in the

[3] Inherent in human beings and above society and its laws.

first paragraph of the preamble of the Universal Declaration and recognised explicitly that, "...dignity inherent in all members of the human family and their equal and inalienable rights constitutes the foundation of freedom, justice and peace in the world." [22] Thus, human dignity became the foundation, the base and the theoretical justification of freedom, justice and peace in the world, serving as the cornerstone of the thirty articles included in that international pact. However, with the recognition of human dignity as the basis of human rights, the problem of its definition arose. At the time the UN Declaration was drafted, this fact led Benedetto Croce to advocate the necessity of holding a formal, international and public debate within which logic, culture and belief would contribute to an agreement on the principles that would be used as the foundation of human dignity [23]. Although this debate might have occurred in part during meetings of the UNESCO Commission for Philosophical Foundations of Human Rights, the clash of the different moralities that were brought to the discussion prevented an agreement that would have led to the establishment of a values-based definition capable of elucidating what constituted human dignity. Consequently, human rights continued to lack a clear foundation in the Universal Declaration. As a result, the rights enshrined in the Universal Declaration were listed generically, awaiting, as Maritain stated [24], a future construction of key values capable of ensuring their understanding and application.

## Practical Application of Human Rights

This generality in the articles of the Universal Declaration of Human Rights has caused serious problems in applying them to concrete cases. Take the example of the situation of Muslim women who wear the burka. This attire was used in ancient times in the region in which Afghanistan and Pakistan are now situated [25], so that noble monarchs would not be seen by commoners [26]. During the Taliban regime (1992-2001), however, the dress became popular and became mandatory in public under the premise that the books and sacred texts of Islam (the Quran, Hadith and Sunnah) required men and women to dress and behave modestly in public [27]. The controversy surrounding this cultural practice lies in the fact that for some Western cultures, it represents a degradation of the dignity of women, relegating women to the role of objects and violating a fundamental human right [28]. On the other hand, wearers of the artifact claim that it is a part of their cultural expression and that they do not feel diminished by the cultural imposition of this moral conduct. By contrast, they feel protected by it and they point to women wearing bikinis in Western beer commercials as real examples of reducing women to mere objects [29]. The arguments presented by both supporters and opponents of the use of the burka, create doubt as to whether this practice is simply a cultural expression of a society's way of realising the human dignity of its members, in accordance with its moral principles. Or, whether it, instead, embodies a subtle form of violation of human dignity by lowering the status of women.

In some Western societies, such as France, wearing the veil is seen as a violation of fundamental human rights. Its use has been banned in public places and accepted only in places of worship (Law No. 524 of 13 July 2010) [30]. The opinion of French culture on the subject is so strong that the law governing the matter states that offenders should receive a fine of one hundred and fifty Euros or compulsory attendance in citizenship classes [31]. According to the French Constitutional Court, which was brought in formally to rule on the matter during an action regarding proposed unconstitutionality, the justification for such rigidity lies in the fact that this is a way of ensuring gender equality for the generation of young Muslims living in France who are forced by their families to wear the burka [32]. The attitude of the French Government led Muslim women in France to protest, arguing that the law was a form of discrimination and disrespect for their culture and that they wanted the right to choose, even if their choice was to wear the burka [33]. The situation created tension because Islam is the second-largest religion in France in terms of practicing members, who represent almost 10 percent of the population [34].

The burka is currently adopted in some Muslim societies under the moral foundation of religion [35]. Its use, however, is not confined to a limited number of countries in the Middle East; according to the Pew Forum on Religion & Public Life, 23.4 percent of the world's population is Muslim. Therefore, of the 6.8 billion current inhabitants of this planet, over 1.6 billion people across the world adopt Muslim beliefs [36]. For certain western groups, however, wearing the veil is seen as a sign of the exclusion and degradation of women and is incompatible with human dignity [37]. In France, for example, the wearing of the veil was banned in public places by Law No. 524 of July 13, 2010 [38]. In the same year, the Senate of Spain approved a motion urging the government to prohibit the wearing of veils that cover the entire face in public places [39]. In April 2010, the Belgian House of Representatives voted to pass a law that would ban the burka and other veils covering the face in public places [40]. In May 2010, in Quebec, Canada, a discussion was begun about Bill No. 94, which contains a proposal to force Muslim women to remove the veil from their faces as a condition for receiving some public services [41]. Around this time, the Vice President of the European Parliament, Silvana Koch-Mehrin, publicly expressed his full support for the ban of the burka in all countries of the European continent [42].

There is no clear explanation in the UN Declaration that dictates whether wearing the veil, or its ban is a violation of human rights. The problem lies in the fact that both the Commission that drafted the Declaration and the scholars who advocated the universality of this category attempted to create a foundation based on a universal morality, which has been perceived by many cultures as cultural imperialism [43].

The solution to this impasse is not, therefore, an attempt to create a universal morality, but the use of a theoretical tool that allows a dialogue between different moralities. Thereafter, the points of contact that can be used as the foundation of human rights can be extracted. To that point, the use of ethics stands out as the most feasible alternative by which to establish this dialogue and overcome the moral barriers that have impeded the realisation of human rights [44]. This choice is justified by the fact that ethics is a branch of philosophy, the purpose of which is the study of moral values, and moral values are the raw material of human rights [45] because they guide the sense of human dignity implementation in every social group. Moreover, this statement challenges us to understand how to develop ethical arguments to conceptualise human rights in the face of the moral diversity in contemporary society.

As an example of this heterogeneity, we may cite Christian, Jewish and Islamic moralities, among others, which establish in different ways the values used as guidelines of conduct for the societies that adopt them. Within this axiological diversity, it is the responsibility of ethics to work with the various moralities, finding points of connection and contact between them, composing and preparing their critiques. In all such situations, the use of ethical reasoning proves to be the most suitable tool for establishing a definition of human rights [46]. Its capacity to engage with various moralities facilitates a multicultural approach and the establishment of values that form the conceptual core of this category of rights, thus removing the risk of its inapplicability in certain cultural contexts.

## Human Dignity As the Ethical Basis of Human Rights

The formulation of an ethical definition of human rights must begin by identifying the core element that forms this class of rights and seeking the ethical value common to all rights that are qualified as elevated to the category of human rights. The Universal Declaration of Human Rights recognised in the first paragraph of its preamble an ethical value to be used as the basis of all rights enshrined there, namely human dignity. Similarly, the various theories that attempt to justify human rights [47] assert, by different arguments and routes, that these rights are ways of realising human dignity, emphasising that this is the core ethical element of this class of rights [48] because they are rooted in the intrinsic value of the dignity found in human beings [49].

According to Immanuel Kant [50], human dignity is a congenital and inalienable quality in all human beings that prevents their objectification. It is embodied through the capacity for self-determination that individuals possess by reason. This quality, however, is also recognised in individuals lacking self-generating conditions, such as young children and people suffering from mental issues because they also have the right to dignified treatment [51]. According to these characteristics, human dignity does not depend on legal recognition [52] because it is an inherent and ethical right placed above cultural specificities and their various morals. It also has the ability to persist even in those societies that do not respect it. Its violation then can be considered to be an affront to the capacity for human self-determination and to the condition of being free.

On the other hand, authors such as Benedetto Croce [53] and Antonio Enrique Pérez-Luño [54] consider the concept of human dignity to be an expanding variable because they understand it as inherent in every historical moment and directed by external human needs for the moral values adopted by each society. The works of Kant, Croce and Pérez-Luño demonstrate that human dignity is best understood when divided into two levels. The first level, which is called the *basic dimension* in this work, is where Kant's theory applies and where the basic legal rights essential to human existence are found—rights that ensure the exercise of each individual's self-determination and prevent his or her objectification. The second level, which is called the *cultural dimension* in this study, encompasses the theories of Croce and Pérez-Luño. This dimension contains the values that vary across time and space and that seek to meet the social demands of each era, in every society, in accordance with their economic, political and cultural capabilities.

Based on these premises, one can see that the basic dimension of human dignity is an inherent quality of the individual that demands respect for life, liberty and physical and moral integrity as the basic rights that prevent the objectification of the human being [55]. Its violation is easily detected in any situation where a person may suffer a reduction of his or her status from a human with rights to a mere instrument or thing that is no longer an end in him or herself.

The cultural dimension, in turn, represents the ways and conditions in which every social group throughout history has implemented human dignity, in its basic dimension. At this level of analysis, space is opened up for cultural peculiarities and practices that vary across time and space, seeking an ethical understanding of the goals of each social group to construct meanings that can be understood cross-culturally [56].

Having acknowledged human dignity and its relation to human rights, one can say that the human rights genus is a set of ethical values, (positive or otherwise) that aim to achieve human dignity in two dimensions. Firstly, a *basic* dimension (protecting individuals against any form of objectification or reduction of their status as humans with rights) and secondly, a *cultural* dimension (protecting moral diversity, represented by different forms as each society implements the basic level of human dignity). This concept associates human rights with a set of ethical values to allow a philosophical discussion of the different existing moralities. In addition, it allows extracting from them common foundations to serve as a cultural approach that, while demanding respect for universal values, protected by these rights through the observance of the basic dimension of human dignity, preserves the moral peculiarities of each social group to develop the cultural dimension of this dignity.

The proposed definition does not attempt to cover legal or moral details to avoid the risk of becoming inapplicable in certain cultural or legislative contexts. Any attempt to conceptualise human rights through the choice of certain moral values would relativise this category because the construction of a uniquely valid or absolute morality is difficult to achieve in the contemporary multicultural context. The definition also omits reference to any rule of law because human rights are supra legal; that is, they are independent of juridical recognition of laws or treaties. Take, for example, freedom, which is regarded in many cultures and in the UN Declaration as belonging to the class of human rights. According to the concept proposed in this work, we can conclude that freedom was recognised as a human right to protect the basic dimension of human dignity because it aims to avoid the objectification of individuals. Imagine a hypothetical society today that did not recognise freedom within its legal system and that allowed slavery. Although under the legal procedure of this social group there would be no violation of the established normative order, there would be a violation of human rights because the basic dimension of human dignity was not achieved: people's status as human beings would be diminished, and they would become mere objects of others' wills.

Thus, we see that the concept proposed here suggests a method for analysing each concrete case, which facilitates the process of identifying human rights by the following parameter: a right is only human when it contains ethical values that represent ways of achieving human dignity, whether in the basic dimension or in the cultural dimension. This conclusion is confirmed by reading the preamble of the Universal Declaration of Human Rights and the 30 articles included in it. The preamble contains the explicit recognition that the rights it describes are based on human dignity. Additionally, an individual analysis of each of the articles shows that they all represent ethical values chosen and recognised as human rights because they represent forms of realising human dignity [57].

## FUNDAMENTAL HUMAN RIGHTS AS A SPECIES OF HUMAN RIGHTS

Within the genus human rights is the category fundamental human rights, which should be understood as a set of ethical values, positive or negative, intended to protect the basic dimension of human dignity. The use of this expression seems appropriate because this is the dimension that contains the list of basic, essential and fundamental legal rights that should be shared by all members of the human species in equal measure without objection [58]. Thus, we see that this basic right is characterised as the minimum foundation required for each society to build the other dimensions of human rights, which in turn represent the different cultural forms of realising human dignity. It should also be noted that this distinction between human rights and fundamental human rights is not intended to relativise the other dimensions of human rights but to uphold the universal basic set of rights that represents the fundamental assertion of human rights. Once implemented and respected, this can serve as the basis for the specification of cultural dignity according to the peculiarities of each group. It is therefore at this level of human rights that the necessary theoretical basis for the universal application of human rights, so desperately sought by the international community in recent decades, may be formed without the risk of relativisation because of cultural specificities.[4]

## The Ethical Concept of Fundamental Human Rights As a Tool for Resolving Specific Cases: The Controversy over Wearing the Veil

Let's return to the issue of the veil for a better understanding of how the ethical concept of fundamental human rights can help in solving real cases.

The wearing of the veil is open to diverse meanings depending on the cultural context in which it is analysed, a fact that has led to conflicting interpretations of its relationship to the human dignity of women. This moral disagreement has occurred mostly because the cultures involved attempt to judge each other's practices using their own value-laden criteria when, in fact, the only way to fairly assess a social behavior is by using the native values-based environment in which it exists.

When analysing the issue of the burka in terms of the two dimensions of human dignity set out in this chapter, we see that in the basic dimension, wearing the veil can only be considered a violation of basic human rights if it significantly reduces the status of the person wearing it *and* if it leads to that person being treated as a mere instrument or object. In this respect, both the imposition of wearing the veil as well as the banning of it embody violations because both positions ignore the rights of women as individuals with their own wishes and the ability to exercise their right to belief and choice. When a culture imposes physical, moral or legal sanctions upon a woman who wears this garment, it reduces her to a mere instrument (object) of the will of others, in violation of the right inherent to all human beings that protects them from being treated as objects. Moreover, the ban on wearing the veil also embodies the degradation of women as humans with rights because it prevents them from exercising their freedom of belief and choice by treating them as incapable of deciding for themselves the kind of life they want to adopt in the pursuit of happiness and fulfillment.

[4] Since the end of World War II, an international effort has aimed to establish a minimum set of rights relating to human dignity that can be applied to all human beings. This effort is evidenced by examination of the declarations and international pacts that emerged from 1948 to 1966: Universal Declaration of Human Rights, the International Covenant on Social Rights and the International Covenant on Civil Rights.

Regarding the analysis of the situation from the aspect of the cultural dimension of human dignity, once the right (fundamental human right) of the woman to choose whether to wear the burka is respected, this practice can be recognised as an expression of the cultural identities adopted by each society. This is possible because this choice represents the free adoption of certain moral values that the wearer of the burka, together with the group in which she exists, chooses for her personal development. Note that at this level of analysis, cultural peculiarities and practices are respected because an ethical understanding is sought of the purposes of each social group without value judgments about the best way to value women or make them happier, because these concepts are, by nature, relative. Thus, the dignity of the woman is respected in its basic dimension and it is also represented by her right to choose. The way she chooses to achieve this dignity is preserved according to the moral values that she elects to follow.

Thus, we can conclude that the position taken by France to ban the use of the burka in public places, based solely on moral values embraced by that society, embodies the attempt to impose a moral/cultural imperialism with total disregard for the beliefs and axioms of women who see wearing the veil as a way to maintain their dignity. The desire displayed by the French government to choose what is right, valid and good for women in its territory based solely and exclusively on a set of morals adopted by most of its nationals represents a flagrant violation of human dignity and disrespect for cultural diversity. The fact is that this prohibition does not take into account that the women who wear the burka out of conviction, and who are treated, in this case, as mere objects, have feelings, desires, dreams and beliefs that must be understood and respected. In this regard, I believe that the Universal Declaration of Human Rights explicitly recognises the right to freedom of religion or belief and its public manifestation [59].

## CONCLUSION

From the perspective of fundamental human rights, the debate over the ban on wearing the veil shows the clash between the desire for universal observance of this class of rights, which has been sought since the proclamation of the Universal Declaration of the UN, and the relativism applied by certain societies that argue for their adaptation to their moral practices. The situation of Muslim women in France is just one example among many others that can be seen daily in the media, where one culture tries to impose a moral vision upon another using the banner of fundamental human rights to justify this practice. Note that the texts of international treaties expressly recognise the freedom of religion and belief, as well as their respective means of externalisation, as a form of the expression of human dignity. However, the absence of a clear and objective foundation for how these rights should be interpreted has led the French government to see the dress worn by Muslim women as contrary to the moral concept of human dignity.

As can be seen in this work, these controversial situations have occurred due to the absence of an understanding of what constitutes fundamental human rights. This is because the concepts developed thus far regarding the generalisation of the texts of international treaties do not clarify the parameters that must be used to identify a right as being human or tell us how these rights must be interpreted.

The theory presented in this chapter proposes the use of ethics and its ability to engage with the various moralities as a tool to conceptualise and build parameters for the identification and interpretation of human rights. In this regard, I would suggest that, through the analysis of the various theories on the subject and by the wording of the preamble of the UN Declaration, that a right might only be considered human when it is based on the realisation of human dignity. It means that this right needs to attend to at least one dimension of human dignity. In the basic dimension, these rights have the aim to protect individuals against any form of objectification or reduction of their status as humans. For this reason, rights fulfilling this basic dimension are called fundamental human rights. In the cultural level of human dignity, the rights aim to further promote rights meeting the basic dimension, respecting the moral forms chosen by each society to implement this dignity.

Thus, when faced with concrete cases such as the ban on wearing the veil in France, any moral benchmarks are replaced by an objective and ethical analysis of facts verifying whether the assessed circumstances imply the degradation of the individuals involved to mere objects, devoid of will. If this degradation is present as in the case studied, it is a clear case of the violation of fundamental human rights. If the practices evaluated, although controversial and incompatible with certain moral readings, do not bring about this degradation, then respect for individuals as humans with rights who are free to follow their beliefs must be protected. These rights are a cultural expression of human dignity.

If the French government simply prohibited Muslim women within its territory from being forced to wear the burka, the conclusion would be different. In this case, there would be a clear respect for the fundamental human right to freedom of choice. The choice of clothing would be seen as a different realisation of the dignity of these women according to the beliefs they have freely chosen to govern their lives.

The theory proposed here allows an objective assessment of individual cases that reconciles relativistic theories with universal ones, as it pursues the universal protection of the basic dimension of human dignity while simultaneously respecting the moral differences adopted by each society.

## REFERENCES


[1] Sarlet, I. W. (2001). Dignidade da Pessoa Humana e Direitos Fundamentais na Constituição Federal de 1988. Porto Alegre: Livraria do Advogado.

[2] Pérez-Luno, A. E. (1999). *Derechos Humanos, Estado de Derecho y Constituicion.* Madrid: Editorial Technos

[3] Leal, R.G. (2000). *Perspectivas Hermenêuticas dos Direitos Humanos e Fundamentais no Brasil.* Porto Alegre: Livraria do Advogado.

[4] Lima Jr.., J. B. (2001). *Os Direitos Humanos Econômicos, Sociais e Culturais*. Rio de Janeiro: Renovar.

[5] Carpinteros-Benitez. F. (1999). Hist*oria del Derecho Natural: um ensayo.* México: Universidad Nacional Autónoma de México.

[6] Rawls, J. B. (2001). *O direito dos Povos*. (L.C. Borges, Trans., pp. 105). São Paulo: Martins Fontes.

[7] Donelly, J. (2003). *Universal Human Rights in Theory and Practice.* New York: Cornell University.

[8] Ishay, M. (2004), *The history of human rights: from ancient times to the globalization era.* California: University of California Press.

[9] Dias, M. C. (2006) Direitos Humanos. In V. *Barreto Dicionário de Filosofia do Direito.* (pp. 246 – 247) Rio de Janeiro: Renovar.

[10] Perez-Luño, A. E. (2001). Concepto y concepción de los derechos humanos: anotaciones a la ponencia de Francisco Laporta. Alicante: Biblioteca Virtual Miguel de Cervantes.

[11] Buergenthal, T. & Shelton, D. (2002). International Human Rights. St. Paul: West Group.

[12] Bobbio, N. (1992). *Era dos Direitos* (C. N. Coutinho, Trans., pp. 25-26). Rio de Janeiro: Campus.

[13] Hobsbawm, E. (2006). *A Era dos Extremos – O Breve Século XX*. (M. Santarrita, Trans., pp. 56-60). São Paulo: Companhia das Letras.

[14] Chacon, M. P. & Cruz, I. F. (2005). Direchos Humanos y Médio Ambiente. In A. H. V. Benjamin & E. Milaré, *Human and Environmental Rights* (pp. 185, 192-193). São Paulo: Revista de Direito Ambietal.

[15] Rodley, N. S. (2002). The Evolution of United Nations' Charter-based Machinery for the Protection of Human Rights, In F. Butler, *Human Rights Protection: Methods and Effectiveness*. (pp. 187-196). Dordrecht (Netherlands): Kluwer Law International

[16] Croce, B. Carr, E. H.(2002). Declarações de Direitos – Benedetto Croce, E. H. Carr, Raymond Aron. Brasília: Senado Federal, Centro de Estudos Estratégicos, Ministério da Ciência e Tecnologia.

[17] Croce, B. Carr, E. H. (2002). Declarações de Direitos – Benedetto Croce, E. H. Carr, Raymond Aron. Brasília: Senado Federal, Centro de Estudos Estratégicos, Ministério da Ciência e Tecnologia.

[18] Unesco (1973), Human Rights: Comments and Interpretations: a symposium. New York: Columbia University Press.

[19] Barreto, V. (2010). O Fetiche dos Direitos Humanos. Rio de Janeiro: Lumen Juris p. 20-21.

[20] Unesco, supra note 20, at p.9. New York: Columbia University Press.

[21] Unesco, supra note 20, at p.17. New York: Columbia University Press.

[22] Ghandhi, P. R. (2004). Internacional Human Rights Documents. Oxford: Oxford University Press, 2002 p. 423.

[23] Unesco, supra note 20, at p.17. New York: Columbia University Press.

[24] Unesco, supra note 20, at p.17. New York: Columbia University Press.

[25] Heath, J. (2008). *The Veil: Women Writers on Its History, Lore and Politics*. Los Angeles: University of California Press.

[26] Kahf, M. (2008). From Her Royal Body the Robe Was Removed: The Blessings of the Veil and the Trauma of Forced Unveilings in the Middle East In J. Heath (Ed.). The Veil: Women Writers on Its History, Lore, and Politics. (pp. 27-43) Los Angeles: University of California Press.

[27] Lyon, D. & Spini, D. (2004). Unveiling the Headscarf Debate. *Feminist Legal Studies,* (12), 338-342.

[28] Tarlo, E. (2010). Visibly Muslim: *Fashion, Politics, Faith. New York:* Oxford 148.

[29] Tarlo, E. (2010). Visibly Muslim: *Fashion, Politics, Faith. New York:* Oxford283.

[30] (2010, Jul 13). *France Parliament approves burka ban..* Retrieved Mar, 28, 2011, from JURIST Legal News & Research: http://jurist.org/paperchase/2010/07/france-parliament-approves-burka-ban.php.

[31] (2010, Oct 7). France constitutional court approves burka ban. Retrieved, Mar, 30 2011, from *JURIST Legal News & Research:* http://jurist.org/paperchase/2010/10/france-constitutional-court-approves-burka-ban.php.

[32] (2010, Oct 12) France. Le Conseil Constitutionnel. Loi interdisant la dissimulation du visage dans l'space public. Décision no 2010 - 613 DC,. Retrieved, Mar, 28, 2011, from Journal officiel du. http://www.conseil-constitutionnel.fr/conseil-constitutionnel/francais/les-decisions/acces-par-date/decisions-depuis-1959/2010/2010-613-dc/decision-n-2010-613-dc-du-07-octobre-2010.49711.html.

[33] (2011, Apr 11) *France Enforces Ban on Full-Face Veils in Public*. Retrieved, Apr, 11, 2011, from The New York Times: http://www.nytimes.com/2011/04/12/world/europe/12france.html?_r=1.

[34] (2010, July 6) That is, approximately six million people, consisting mostly of immigrants from former French colonies in Africa such as Tunisia, Algeria and Morocco. *Marseille's Muslims eye long-awaited mosque.* Retrieved, Mar, 28, 2011, from BBC News: http://www.bbc.co.uk/news/10508069.

[35] Lyon, D. & Spini, D. The Headscarf Debat. *Feminist Legal Studies, Netherlands,* supra note 29, 342.

[36] The Future of the Global Muslim Population: Projections for 2010-2030, Retrieved, Apr, 13, 2011, from Pew Forum on Religion & Public Life: http://pewforum.org/The-Future-of-the-Global-Muslim-Population.aspx.

[37] (2011, Mar, 13) Full-Face Veils Outlawed as France Spells Out Controversial Niqab Ban. Retrieved Mar, 28, 2011, from The Guardian: http://www.guardian.co.uk/world/2011/mar/03/niqab-ban-france-muslim-veil.

[38] (2010, July, 13) France Parliament Approves Burka Ban. Retrieved, Mar, 28, 2011, from JURIST Legal News & Research:, http://jurist.org/paperchase/2010/07/france-parliament-approves-burka.

[39] (2010, June, 23) Spain Senate Calls For Government Ban of Face Veils. Retrieved, Apr, 6, 2011, from JURIST Legal News & Research:http://jurist.org/paperchase/2010/06/spain-senate-calls-for-government-ban-of-face-veils.php

[40] Projet de loi visant à interdire le port de tout vêtement cachant totalement ou de manière principale le visage. Retrieved, Apr, 6, 2011, from La Chambre des représentants et le Sénat:http://www.dekamer.be/kvvcr/showpage.cfm?section=/questure&language=fr&story=building.xml&rightmenu=right

[41] (2010, May 28) No Consensus at Quebec Niqab Hearings.Retrieved, Apr, 6, 2011, from CBC News: http://www.cbc.ca/news/canada/montreal/story/2010/05/18/niqab-hearings-quebec.html.

[42] (2010, May 2) Europe Parliament VP Calls for Continent-Wide Burka Ban. Retrieved, Apr, 6, 2011, from, JURIST Legal News & Research: http://jurist.org/paperchase/2010/06/spain-senate-calls-for-government-ban-of-face-veils.php.

[43] Rocha, L. S. & Streck, L. (2003). *Anuário do Programa de Pós-Graduação em Direito: Mestrado e Doutorado.* São Leopoldo: Unisinos.

[44] Saldaña, J. (1999). Notas sobre la fundamentación de los derechos humanos. México: Boletín Mexicano de Derecho comparado, Universidad Nacional Autónoma de México.

[45] Janusz Symonides, (2000). *Human Rights: concepts and standards.* Aldershot: Ashgate / UNESCO p. 31.

[46] Campos, G. J. B. (1993). *Teoria General de los Derechos Humanos.* Ciudad Universitaria: Universidad Nacional Autónoma de México, p. 82.

[47] Baez, N. L. X. & Barretto, V. (2007). *Direitos Humanos e Globalização.* Joaçaba: Editora Unoesc, p. 18.

[48] Fernandez, E. (1991). *Teoria de la Justicia y Derechos Humanos.* Madrid: Debate. p. 78.

[49] Flood, P. J. (1998). *The Effectiveness of UN Human Rights Institutions.* Westport: Praeger Publishers.

[50] Kant, I. (1980). Fundamentação da Metafísica dos Costumes. IN I. Kant, Os pensadores (P. Quintela, Trans., PP. 134-5; 140-1.) São Paulo: Abril Cultural.

[51] Dworkin, R. (2003). O Domínio da Vida: Aborto, Eutanásia e Liberdades Individuais ( J. L. Camargo, Trans., PP. 309-10.) São Paulo: Martins Fontes

[52] Martinez, A. A. (1996). La Dignidad de la Persona como Fundamento del Ordenamiento Constitucional Espanol. Léon: Universidad di Léon.

[53] Croce, B. (2002) Declarações de Direito. Brasília: Senado Federal, Centro de Estudos Estratégicos, Ministério da Ciência e Tecnologia.

[54] Pérez-Luño, A. E. (1984). Derechos Humanos em la Sociedade Democratica, p. 48.

[55] Sarlet, I. W. (2005). As Dimensões da Dignidade da Pessoa Humana: Construindo uma Compreensão Jurídico-Constitucional Necessária e Possível. In I. W. Sarlet, Dimensões da dignidade: ensaios de filosofia do direito e direito constitucional (PP. 37-38) Porto Alegre: Livraria do Advogado.

[56] Höffe, O. (2005). *A Democracia no Mundo de Hoje* (T. L. C. Romão, Trans.), (PP. 77-78) São Paulo: Martins Fontes.

[57] Baez, N. L. X. (2010). Dimensões de Aplicação e Efetividade dos Direitos Humanos. In Congresso Nacional do CONPEDI. Florianópolis: Anais do XIX Congresso Nacional do CONPEDI.

[58] Flores, J, H. (2009). *A (Re)invenção dos Direitos Humanos*.(C. R. D. Garcia & A. Suxberger & J. A. Dias, Trans.) (pp. 29). Florianópolis: Fundação Boiteux.

[59] Universal Declaration of Human Rights, G.A. Res. 217A, U.N. GAOR, 3d Sess., 1st plen. mtg., U.N. Doc. A/810 (Dec. 12, 1948).

In: International Perspectives of Multiculturalism ISBN: 978-1-63483-971-6
Editor: Ornette D. Clennon 

*Chapter 4*

# THE BLACK FACE OF EUROCENTRISM: UNCOVERING GLOBALISATION

***Ornette D. Clennon*** [*]
**Manchester Metropolitan University, Manchester, UK**

## ABSTRACT

In this chapter, using Frantz Fanon and Jacques Lacan, Ornette D Clennon attempts to trace the hidden psychopathological structures of globalisation.

Clennon refutes the idea of the heterogeneous effects of globalisation as he traces how it uses 'whiteness' as both a homogenising and hegemonising tool of market conformity. Clennon also argues that globalisation is essentially both an economic and cultural discourse that generates heterogeneous market forms of 'whiteness', which are decoupled from specific racial loci but are nevertheless embedded within the market concept of "individuality," itself a tool of social control.

**Keywords:** globalisation, 'whiteness', 'blackness', market, individuality, cultural memory, psychopathology, Lacan, Fanon

[*] E-mail: o.clennon@mmu.ac.uk.

# INTRODUCTION

In Chapter 2, I introduced the "militarisation of culture" as a concept that uses a Huntingdon-influenced international cultural memory as the ethical basis upon which to prosecute the 'war on terror' and to constitute an 'international community'. In this chapter, I will examine a 'soft' (but equally dangerous) form of global power and identify its cultural pervasiveness, which acts to prepare the ground for the concept of 'hard' geopolitical power in Chapter 2.

## Cultural Memory and Globalisation

The idea of cultural memory is important here because not only does is it involve the forming of macro-narratives about stakeholdership and belonging, as explored in Chapter 2, it also informs the micro-narratives behind the construction and global transmission of 'cultural products'[1]. Elsewhere, I introduce the concept of Afro Neo Romanticism [1] where I describe how commercial Eurocentric or Americocentric 'cultural memories' continue to shape the world via a powerful form of cultural commodification and globalisation. The cultural memories to which I am particularly referring are those that have been commercialised from the era that produced an African Diaspora via the transatlantic commerce route. In an American context, this is important because much of America's global cultural exports in popular culture are founded on (commercial) expressive art forms originally created by diasporic African Americans. However, Revathi Krishnaswarmy [2] (p. 108) reminds us that, "corporate globalization is thriving precisely by emptying out the subversive potential in culture." This point is key in understanding how the historical *and* cultural memories of the original African American art forms and their subversive meanings have been stripped back to a commercial husk whose signifiers are able to globally export cultural products as market commodities.

[1] In many ways, I appear to be prefiguring the globalisation concepts of the local and the global ('glocal'), as will be discussed later. However, here, on one hand, I am specifically referring to the macro-narratives that inform and are informed by both national and international cultural memories, as explored in Chapter 2. On the other hand, I am also referring to the micro-narratives that infuse cultural products with the power to help build and transmit cultural memories, in so doing, in aggregate, enabling the conveying of macro-narratives and their cultural memories.

For me what is interesting is not only how globalisation occurs and how it is transformed or translocated[2] [3, 4] to other cultural traditions, but how it still manages to homogenise the cultures to which it is transferred. Of course, this point about the process of homogenisation is controversial, as many scholars believe that globalisation is a force for 'vernacularisation' [5] and heterogeneity [6-12], where external cultures are moulded and adapted to local indigenous cultures and in the process, creating culturally subversive and hegemonic forms[3] [13]. However, like Herbert Schiller [14] and others [15, 16], I tend to take a less optimistic view of this type of neoliberal cultural re-invention because the cultural objects being subversively subsumed into the host cultures nevertheless still, "bear the ideological imprint of the main centers of the capitalist world economy" (p. 10) according to Schiller. This idea of the imprint is resonant for me. If we accept Krishnaswarmy's image of the, "emptying out the subversive potential in culture" or as I characterised it elsewhere, 'decoupling the historical memories from the cultural object' [17] leaving us with a mere commercial husk or "shell" as Walter Benjamin [18] might call it, then the vernacularised cultural object still bears the original imprint of the external culture. This imprint can be characterised in two ways. Firstly, if we ascribe to the view that mass cultural dissemination serves to deterritorialise mass cultural production, which in turn weakens the concept of the "nation-state" [19, 20], we fail to acknowledge the inherent systemic power of the very infrastructures that are needed to 'transport' (deterritorialise) mass cultural production across the globe. And that they are in themselves edifices to neoliberal marketeering and (post-modern cultural) economics. As an example, in Chapter 2, Tavia N'yong'o [21] reminded us that the instantaneity of global communications can easily dupe us into thinking that

[2] I am alluding to the process Walter Benjamin describes when he refers to the "anamnestic intoxication" (of the flânerie [stroll]) where "abstract knowledge" of the city (Paris) masquerading as "something experienced and lived through" is communicated "person to person, especially by word of mouth" (p. 417) and re-invented as lived (authentic) experiences in the new individual. Here Benjamin's idea of external and multiple psychic interior re-inventions that are not experienced by the new flâneur, very much prefigures Edward Said's concept of the Traveling Theory, where for Said theories/texts can be transformed between readings like a game of Chinese whispers resulting in processes of indigenisation and hybridisation that work to de-stabilise the original (Western) source.

[3] Stuart Hall reminds us that, [S]tructured in dominance [globalisation]… cannot control or saturate everything within its orbit. Indeed, it produces as one of its unintended effects subaltern formations and emergent tendencies which it cannot control but must try to hegemonize or harness to its wider purposes. It is [a] system for con-forming difference, rather than a convenient synonym for the obliteration of difference (p. 215).

our consumption of cultural products creates 'glocal'[4] [22-25], solidarity and agency when for the most part all it succeeds in doing is being monetised as user-generated content and contributing to the process of capital accumulation [26, 27]. N'yong'o calls this "Participation as Neoliberal Fantasy" (p. 52). So already, this vernacularisation process of heterogeneous 'contrapuntal meanings'[5] [28, 29] falls prey to the asymmetric balance of power in the area of how cultural products are exported (globalised) and so cannot help but be tinged by a subliminal neoliberal structural imprint.

However, as I have already hinted, when we examine the "unique endowments" of the cultural product[6], we can begin to re-define its 'uniqueness' in terms of the cultural and historical memories it carries. As an example, if we look at the cultural product that is cricket and its post-colonial export, Derek Birley as cited by Brett St Louis [30] describes the game as, "not so much a game as institutionalised nostalgia" (p. 180). Here, what is implied is how the game of cricket became synonymous with class and socio economic standing. Cricket originally was only played by English gentlemen with the socio economic status to afford (in terms of time) such a leisure pursuit. Even within the game itself, strokes such as the "off drive" became associated with a class-driven *bodily* aesthetic of 'grace'. Being able to play such a technically difficult shot of power but make it look effortless became a symbolic ideal of civilised *(genteel)* Victorian masculinity; the stroke literally embodying imperial aspirations of control *and* power. So not only did the game of cricket serve to physically represent the qualities of colonial rule by

---

[4] When discussing the relationship between the effects of the global and the local, Roland Robertson in this context, talks about "global culture" (p. 31), whilst Erik Swyngedouw talks about "socio-spatial power choreographies" (p. 26). However, Krishnaswarmy warns us that it would be foolhardy to ignore these at best hegemonising, at worst homogenising properties of glocalism or as Doreen Massey would characterise them, "power geometries" (p. 149); a similar process to the description in Chapter 2 of forging national cultural memories into a composite international cultural memory that serves the Americanisation of international relations.

[5] Rather tellingly Edward Said in his *Culture and Imperialism* concedes this point (p. 7): It is difficult to connect these different realms, to show the involvements of culture with expanding empires, to make observations about art that preserve[s] its unique endowments and at the same time map its affiliations, but, I submit, we must attempt this, and set the art in the global, earthly context.

Here, Said implies a tension between the intrinsic properties of the cultural product and its need to negotiate its "affiliations" with its means of transmission, representation, translation and consumption. However, when the intrinsic nature of the cultural product has been (apparently) removed leaving just its "affiliations", we are left with the prospect of its absent "intrinsicality" (imprint) dictating its terms of affiliation from afar like, "attitudes of a dominating metropolitan center ruling a distant territory" (p. 9).

[6] See note 4.

creating a cultural memory of Empire that was easily and visually understood, the game itself became an institutional repository of tradition designed to perpetuate nostalgic imperial symbolic representation. I could argue, as does Arjun Appadurai [31], that cricket in India has been totally 'vernacularised' by virtue of its expression in a liminal space, where it represents neither the colonised or coloniser, in this vernacularised context. However, I am still perplexed by his observation of cricket as being, "an emblem of Indian nationhood at the same time that it became inscribed, as practice, onto the Indian (male) body" (p. 112). For me, despite all of the collectivist deconstruction of British imperialism in cricket's symbolism, what was actually being vernacularised was the *power* and *control* of the 'colonial institution', in other words, cricket's "unique endowments" being "mapped" onto its "affiliations," in this case, the Indian *male body*. Already in cricket's original Victorian English setting, the visual male bodily aesthetic of grace and 'absent' power was commonly understood to be a quintessential ideal of a patriarchal British Empire. So, despite vernacular attempts at using (a now liminal form of) cricket to overcome national caste divisions and the effects of British colonialism, the "emblem of Indian nationhood" was still apparently very much shaped by Victorian British patriarchal values that were mapped onto the Indian male body, which rather re-enforced local patriarchal value systems. This for me represents a form of cultural homogenisation not the (idealistic) heterogeneous, hybridising qualities of the global cultural export[7] [32].

So, using cricket as a brief example, we can see just how difficult it is to divest the imported cultural product of its "unique endowments". As outlined earlier, this is made all the more difficult not just because of the stubborn persistence of its "unique endowments" but also because of the asymmetric power balance of its "affiliations" (e.g., post-modern mass production, communications and exports). I agree with Stuart Hall [33] when he describes, a complex process of hegemony where "structured dominance" (p. 215) seeks to conform any vernacularised subaltern resistance to its wider will. However, I would characterise this further as a psychological battle within the globalised

[7] Michael Dusche gives a thorough historical account of India's indigenous ethical ambivalence towards the personal agency of the female body by exploring traditional Indian hierarchical ethics and contemporary Indian feminist egalitarian morality. So, of course, I would not in any way blame India's acculturation of cricket for their historical battles for women's rights. I would, however, tentatively argue that the high colonial status of a male dominated cricket with its embedded patriarchal values would have, on some level, emboldened or strengthened indigenous disregard for individual female agency (a sort of 'if it's good enough for them, it's good enough for us' mindset).

(colonised) subject where even though they are indigenising the "unique endowments" of the cultural product they are still profoundly shaped by it at the same time. So even though the cultural product might appear to have been utterly transformed into a (subversive) native cultural form, it still will have been hailed into *being* performatively [34] by the (power of the) cultural import.

This performative process finds the vernacularised cultural product re-presenting the now 'forgotten/absent' power of the imported cultural product as its (native) own. On the surface, this might seem like a heterogeneous proliferation of new cultural identities existing in a liminal third space but for me, the stubborn oppressive power of the imposed cultural product still remains but only now deeply internalised by the subject [35].

***Afro Neo Romanticism***

This leads me back to my discussion about the globalising/colonising power of Afro Neo Romanticism (ANR), as a cultural product. Firstly, as mentioned earlier, its "unique endowments" have been stripped away leaving an empty husk that is ripe for global commercial exploitation. However, the imprint of its 'endowments' are present and from afar they still manage to infiltrate native attempts at subversion. Secondly, ANR is founded on a historical cultural discourse visually and conceptually represented by the Black (fe)male body and its representation of power and control. However, before going on to explore the psychopathology of ANR and why it is important to examine it through this lens, I would like to give the briefest of summaries of what constitutes Afro Neo Romanticism.

Elsewhere [36], I write at length about the metaphorical (surface) borrowings of ANR from German literary Romanticism in terms of ANR's actualised Kantian metaphysics of life and death and its urban translocation of the German woods and forests as places of magic.

I argue that the African American popular cultural export that is Hip Hop uses life and death as near-phenomenological analyses of ghetto life and portrays the ghetto itself as a place of mysticism and magic[8] [37-39]. As a

[8] I am particularly reminded of the seminal 1994 Illmatic album by Nas, who explicitly describes the precarious nature of living in a 'ghetto' where life is commoditised as a function of drugs-distribution and its resultant accumulation of capital. In critiquing Michael Eric Dyson & Sohail Daulatzai's 'hip-hop-against-racism'-reading of the social themes in Illmatic, Demetrius Noble observes the importance of being able to locate the asymmetric balances of power behind commercial hip hop that allows it, as Stuart Hall would say, to 'conform' authentic African American resistance (to commercial exploitation) to its dominant market ideologies and its ensuing cultural products.

global 'Romantic' holding concept, Afro Neo Romanticism fuses music with 'urban' style and culture[9] [40] to sell a fantasy representation of "Blackness"[10] [41] that glamorises the 'ghetto life'[11] [42]. Afro Neo Romanticism's "unique endowments", in this case, consists of a mix of cultural memories that institutionalises historical and oppressive stereotyping[12] [43] and the innovative African American (music) art forms of resistance stemming from their oppression [44].

The form that these endowments take is the Black male body (the image as well as the concept) onto which all of these cultural memories are mapped and which in itself becomes fetishised into an object of desire. My argument is that the "unique endowments" or the cultural memories of the Black male body have been stripped away leaving a commercial representation of the Black male body that is able to sell other products in a market of commoditised culture. However, the sad pun of Edward Said's "unique endowments" is that they have not been entirely removed, as their imprint on the cultural product (visual, cultural and conceptual merchandising of "blackness") is still felt.

---

[9] Elsewhere, I discuss subcultural and post subcultural studies within the context of Birmingham's (UK) Centre for Contemporary Cultural Studies (1964-2002), where the former's preoccupation with research into the relationship between culture, consumption and socio economic status was replaced with studies around the semiotics of style and kinship networks formed from shared interests in 'style'. However, the point I make is that both areas of study are two sides of the same coin because post subcultural studies still assumes a level of socio economic privilege that enables the subject to consume culture in an ephemeral way. Subcultural studies, on the other hand, looks at how the subject uses culture as a means of active resistance against the effects of capitalist exclusion. Both forms of studies in their own ways examine the function of the markets in the commodification of culture.

[10] On the commercial exoticisation of "blackness", Tellef Kvifte writes:

> From this perspective it makes sense to consider ethnicity as a feature on its own, detached from specific ethnic groups: the 'general ethnic' property that is tied to a certain type of exoticism where one is looking for 'the credible alien'. In the global Romantic Movement, street credibility is traded for forest credibility.
>
> But connecting the 'ethnic' to the 'exotic' has its pitfalls. In a sense, 'being ethnic' is reserved for other people, as the path to credibility and authenticity I see this as the modernist tragedy: the hunt for a credible authentic identity that becomes like the hunt for the gold at the end of the rainbow. As you move towards it, it slips further away. (paras. 29, 30).

[11] I am particularly thinking of "ghetto fabulousness" which is a concept that transforms the effects of structural urban poverty into a post subcultural facet of 'style'.

[12] In his Black Reconstruction in America 1860-1880 W.E.B Du Bois rebuts the pervasive attitudes towards "Negroes" that were widely taught in the US educational establishment at the beginning of the twentieth century. They included; Negroes are lazy, Negroes are dishonest and extravagant and Negroes make bad governments.

## The Psychopathology of 'Whiteness'

In order to better understand the nature of Said's "unique endowments" and their tenacious refusal to relinquish their 'absent' control over their 'emptied out' cultural product, we might need to incorporate a psychoanalytical tone to our discussion that will help to elucidate the stubborn psychical components (endowments) of Afro Neo Romanticism [45]. Derek Hook [46] makes a persuasive argument for borrowing elements of the psychological when discussing issues that concern the political. Hook uses the psychoanalytical writings of Frantz Fanon [47, 48] and the political writings of Steve Biko [49, 50] to illustrate the often symbiotic relationship between these two areas of discourse. In this section, I will also use a psychoanalytical tone to frame some of my political discourses around the representation of the Black body and its meanings. But first, I will introduce the concept of 'Whiteness' and outline why it is so important that it is identified.

Very much taking my cue from Toni Morrison's *Playing in the Dark: Whiteness and the Literary Imagination* [51], I was struck by her observation that, "[t]he fabrication of an Africanist persona is reflexive, an extraordinary meditation of the self; a powerful exploration of fears and desires that reside in the…conscious" (p. 17).

Here, Morrison is not using the term "Africanist" in the way that the African philosopher, Valentin Mudimbe [52] is when he categorises the development of African philosophy[13]. Morrison uses the term to describe the 'imprint' (or its aftershock) of Africans and African Americans on the psyche of White America. Through the literary criticism of key American texts, Morrison uncovers a form of "whiteness" whose very existence is dependent on a construct of "blackness" in order to survive. This co-dependence between the concepts of "whiteness" and "blackness" very much reminds me of Friedrich Hegel's Master/Slave (Lordship and Bondage) dialectic [53] of self-consciousness, where the Master depends on his slave to recognise him as the

[13] Mudimbe believes that the "knowledge" (gnosis; redolent of the concepts, 'spiritual' and 'self-revelatory/actualising') contained in (Sub-Saharan) African philosophy is not easily attained as it remains partially obscured by Eurocentric enquiry. Mudimbe attempts to deconstruct or excavate the Foucauldian power matrices that determine the deeper levels of knowledge-mediation and knowledge-origin (epistemology) in order to arrive at an Afrocentric view of Africa rather than a Eurocentric one. In order to achieve this, Mudimbe thoroughly deconstructs the shifting relationship between Europe and the African "Other" over the centuries by using an approach he calls, "dynamic anthropology" (p. 184). This is an extension of what he calls the current phase of 'critically reflective philosophy' the product of two previous phases of African philosophy namely; The 'Political' (ideological) and The 'Ethnological' (anthropological).

Master whilst the slave's self-affirmation comes from his work as the recogniser (serving the needs of the Master). This seems to be crucial in this dialectic as the Master is actually enslaved by his need for recognition (the fantasy of Mastery) which can only be provided by the slave's work, whilst the slave is liberated by his work, as it is his work that validates him, not his Master.

With this dialectic in mind, Morrison very much implies that the White American psyche, in order to achieve self-efficacy and agency, attaches to itself and *privileges* notions of freedom and 'Mastery'. It in turn, needs an *unacknowledged* but equally powerful opposite of "blackness," with corresponding notions of a lack of agency and 'enslavement' to self-actualise or hail its "whiteness" (freedom) and agency into being[14]. For example, in Mark Twain's *The Adventures of Huckleberry Finn* [54], Morrison observes that the character of the runaway (black) slave only serves to emphasise the protagonist's freedom as a white man. Here, the 'blackness' of Jim is exactly what highlights or shapes/hails into being the (American) *ideal* of Huck's 'whiteness' by throwing into contrast the seemingly dialectical positions of 'whiteness and freedom' and 'blackness and enslavement'. What is interesting for me is the implied process of performativity, where Huck's "whiteness" was brought into being by Jim's "blackness" throughout the novel but is somehow never fully determined as 'real' because at the end of the novel, we discover that Jim was actually also a *free* man. Morrison suggests that the novel's ending with the reader being unable to follow Huck's adventures into the territories (representing his full self-actualisation as a free *white* man) was disrupted by the fact that his "whiteness" was only ever a fantasy based on a dialectical position that had never existed. Using Huckleberry Finn as an example, Morrison shows us that Africanism could be perceived as another way of perceiving Said's "unique endowments" that are mapped onto their "affiliations" in this case (the concept of) 'blackness'. So if we can begin to

[14] Morrison's point about the association between freedom and 'whiteness' and an implicit 'blackness' and enslavement starts with the observation that European settlers arrived in America looking for religious freedoms but also freedoms from European (especially British) constraints of class and tradition. Morrison explains that their desire for freedom did not make them immune from the "terror of human freedom" (p. 37). I interpret this terror as a kind of moral panic along the lines of 'what are we going to do with all of this self-determination and freedom after being so used to the societal constraints of our previous home land?' In order to assuage this panic, Morrison asserts that the early settlers needed to 'invent' (to other) a group of people whom they could enslave in order to reconstitute a social order to which they were more psychically used. So 'blackness' to them became synonymous with enslavement for the whole purpose of giving them a much needed anchor or structure for their new psychic freedoms of 'whiteness'.

think of 'blackness' as an unacknowledged psychic function of 'whiteness', existing purely to enable 'whiteness' to exist, we can begin to appreciate the pathology of what is largely a near-invisible process of Africanist subjectivation, as Neil Altman [55] explains:

> What makes the fantasy of whiteness a pathological defense is the way it is paired with blackness as its disavowed double. The search for mastery becomes problematic when it becomes so desperate that it must entail the construction of a subjected group of people and the disavowal of one's own helplessness— i.e., when the experience of helplessness is warded off, rather than integrated with the experience of mastery...history provides abundant examples of how the fantasy of mastery has taken the form of mastery of other people, a sadomasochistic, dominant-submissive form. This fantasy has been actualized in the form of colonialism, slavery, discrimination in housing, access to employment and education, and in myriad other forms of prejudice (p. 57).

I would add that it is precisely this pathological "fantasy of whiteness" that has been institutionalised, marketised and globalised as a homogenising cultural commodity in the form of Afro Neo Romanticism about which I have previously written at great length [56].

### *The Fantasy of 'Whiteness'*

The most enduring symbol of 'blackness' can be found in the commercial representation of the black male body. In fact, since the image of the black male body is constituted through an inverted male gaze [57][15], I will deliberately gender 'whiteness' as male in the following analyses[16] [58]. If we

---

[15] According to Maurice Patterson and Richard Elliott, "when the gaze is turned on itself, men are more likely to move through a range of responses such as rejection, identification and desire" (p. 241).

[16] It is outside of the scope of this chapter to fully explore the intersectional nature of oppression with the construct of a racial patriarchy that privileges white, heterosexual, able-bodied, cis-gendered maleness but Patricia Hill Collins fully explores this using her concept of the "matrix of domination" (p. 18). However, in distinguishing between intersectionality and matrices of domination, Collins writes (p. 18):

I use and distinguish between both terms in examining how oppression affects Black women. Intersectionality refers to particular forms of intersecting oppressions, for example, intersections of race and gender, or of sexuality and nation. Intersectional paradigms remind us that oppression cannot be reduced to one fundamental type, and that oppressions work together in producing injustice. In contrast, the matrix of domination refers to how these intersecting oppressions are actually organized. Regardless of the particular intersections involved, structural, disciplinary, hegemonic, and interpersonal domains of power reappear across quite different forms of oppression.

accept that this 'blackness' is actually a function of 'whiteness'[17] [59], what is this saying about the 'fantasy of (male) whiteness'? Elsewhere [60], I have written at length about how visual depictions of 'blackness' reduce "black men not only to bodies… but also to body parts, especially the penis" [61] (p. 161): the archetypal commercial construct of hypermasculine 'blackness' with his oiled up, high-contrast photographed, muscular torso. Since so many commentators (e.g., [62-65]) have thoroughly examined the fetishisation of the black male form, its sexual objectification and the psychic violence enacted against it through the process of dehumanisation (and control), I will not rehearse these well-known concepts, here. I will just add that the historical relationship between 'whiteness' and 'blackness', as discussed earlier, is mostly mapped onto this archetypal visual image/concept. However, what interests me is a possible psychological explanation of why these images/concepts and their "affiliations" exist so powerfully within the racial animus of male 'whiteness'.

If we accept the construction of male 'whiteness' as a form of subjectivation, we can begin to transpose Hegel's 'Master/Slave' dialectic, as described earlier (that explores the perception of "the self from the self-perspective" [66] (p. 126)) to the perception of 'whiteness from its self-perspective'. For me, how 'self' and in this case, 'whiteness' splits into the antithetical positions of "I" and "Other" is interesting. This for Jacques Lacan [67] is the necessary tension that forms the building block of the 'self' through the process of alienation. From here, read 'whiteness' for the 'self' (subject). For Lacan, alienation occurs when the subject realises that it is dependent on the affirmation of an "other" (e.g., the infant's own reflection in a mirror or its mother) for its self-realisation yet is still a *rival* of the "other" for its intrinsic distinctiveness. This is because the bodily reflection of the infant (that looks whole and complete) does not match up to its felt fragmented bodily experiences (e.g., of bodily motor un-coordination). So, there is an aggressive tension in the infant because the image serves to threaten the infant with fragmentation (i.e., forcing it to see itself as un-coordinated). The infant in effect becomes a rival with its own image but in order to win, it chooses the image as its 'ideal self' (imago) and proceeds to identify with its reflection and strives to become its 'ideal self' over its lifetime. Lacan characterises this as the Mirror stage in child development and very much sees this as the natural development of the ego.

---

[17] Frantz Fanon, observing, "that what is often called the black soul is a white man's artifact" (p. 6).

Transposed to dialectical white 'maleness', the former sees black 'maleness' as its 'complete' reflection (in the imaginary mirror) but this black 'maleness' creates a tension within white 'maleness' because it cannot quite match up its own experience of 'fragmented' maleness [68][18] with its perception of 'whole/complete' black maleness that is being reflected back at it. This 'aggressive tension' (a term Lacan identifies as having an erotic component) finally abates with white 'maleness' adopting black 'maleness' as its reflection or 'ideal self' which it strives to become (and *master*, my addition[19]) Lacan also says that the infant's 'ideal self' is haunted by the memory of feeling 'fragmented' and this anxiety manifests itself in images of dismemberment, mutilation and dislocation. Lacan asserts that long after the mirror stage, these anxieties coalesce around the penis and castration. This, for me, casts the fetishisation of the 'black male body' into an interesting light, as we can begin to see its fragmentation and penile fascination[20] as a projected fear of white (fragmented) 'maleness'[21]. Furthermore, the actual historical lynchings and castrations of the black male body can be viewed as a neurosis[22] of white 'maleness' born out of a disavowed anxiety of fragmentation (castration). After all of this, we can see that the function of 'whiteness' ('self') continues to be expressed through the same positionalities of "I" and

---

[18] Going back to Toni Morrison's observations about the European settlers; even though they had left patriarchal societies their sense of masculinity could still have been 'fragmented' due the constraints of religion, class and tradition that they had left behind. For example, we can get a sense of this feeling of 'fragmentation' from the ideas of the influential writer, Edward Long, who in his 1774 book, *The History of Jamaica, Volume 2*, famously cited Africans as having, "no plan or system of morality among them" (p. 353). For Long, the perceptions of their 'native' customs seemed, to him, so alien to the British patriarchal system that they could only have been possibly perceived as 'immoral' in sharp contrast to the "morality" left behind in England. See Chapter 2 for a fuller discussion about how these 'forgotten' ideas became historically embedded in the psyches of British society and her institutions.

[19] I think in this transposition, 'master' might be a more accurate term for this process of identification, as Altman already recognises the "search for mastery" as a pathological function of 'whiteness'.

[20] As Collins observes, earlier, that there is a reduction of "black men not only to bodies….. but also to body parts, especially the penis."

[21] Interestingly, if 'whiteness' as Neil Altman suggested earlier, were to integrate its "experience of helplessness" with its "experience of mastery" so that a "We" was constructed instead of an "I" and "Other", (male) 'whiteness' and its need for its disavowed opposite of the "Other" would cease to exist. See Chapter 5 for an interesting take on this integrative approach from the view of 'constructing' Koreanness.

[22] Depending on whether we ascribe to the Freudian meaning of neurosis as an illness to be cured or the Lacanian meaning that describes neurosis as 'normal' mental health (i.e., statistically most common in the human population), where mental health is just an illusion we follow to help us get over the fact that our self-actualisation is split (alienation and separation), will determine whether we take an optimistic or pessimistic view of 'whiteness'!

"Other" but with the question: What do "I" want/need[23] [69-72]? This question is the point of self-interest 'whiteness' needs in order to survive because being homogenised into an unconscious collective or even an open ended plurality would represent the death of 'whiteness' (i.e., Morrison's, "terror of human freedom"!) Interestingly, Frantz Fanon [73] in his *Black Skin, White Masks* explores the psychology of gendered ''blackness' from its self-perspective'. Fanon also perceiving a dialectic but from the view of the colonised subject asks the strikingly similar question, "What does the blackman want?" (p. 1) and concludes, "[t]he black man wants to be white. The whiteman slaves to reach a human level" (p. 3). Fanon's answer to this question fascinates me because in effect both the 'blackman' and the 'whiteman' want to "reach a

[23] The distinction between need and want will be explored later. However, Lacan does use Freud's Oedipal Complex as a starting point for describing the separation of 'desires' after the 'self' has been defined (via the alienation process) . Lacan describes the situation where the infant realises that it is not the ultimate object (Phallus) of its Mother's affection, which means that the satisfaction of the Mother's affection has to come from elsewhere, outside of the infant and from the Father. The Child at this point also realises that the Mother seeks ultimate satisfaction from elsewhere, so does not, herself, have the Phallus. Lacan uses Father in the context of a symbolic (not real) signifier of the "Other", in other words that which lies outside of the dyadic relationship of Mother and Child. More precisely, Lacan posits that the Father possesses the Phallus which can only satisfy the Mother, again a symbolic signifier (in the strictly Lacanian sense). This is crucial because the Child realises that it does not possess (nor is) the Phallus so the child asks itself what the Mother wants from it, if it cannot satisfy her with 'the' Phallus it does not possess. Separation (of desires) for Lacan, occurs when the Child realises that its desires differ from that of its Mother. Lacan conjects that the Child's realisation that it neither owns nor is the Phallus constitutes a symbolic castration of the Child; the first castration being that of the Mother when the Child realises that she does not have the Phallus, either. Lacan says that this castration (the realisation of lack) is necessary for the healthy development of an individual (although he recognises that it is not possible to fully accept this castration, as desire or the search for the Phallus, remains) but this is the 'norm', by degree). However, Lacan believes that the root of psychopathological structures is castration (a lack/search for satisfaction). If a subject is mildly neurotic, Lacan says this shows that the subject is repressing its awareness of castration (lack) because, "it is the assumption of castration that creates the lack on the basis of which desire is instituted" (p. 852). However, when the subject denies that castration (or a lack) ever existed at all, Lacan asserts that as a result of this symbolic disavowal, castration can occur in the real world through hallucinations of dismemberment or actual genital mutilation. Now, in terms of possibly locating white male 'desire', this puts the historical real world lynchings of blackmen against which Ida B Wells-Barnett so tirelessly campaigned, into stark contrast. Wells-Barnett already hints at some sort of white male disavowal when she notes, "that the world has accepted the story that the Negro is a monster which the Southern white man has painted him" (p. 36). However, Frantz Fanon goes even further and asks, Still on the genital level, when a white man hates black men, is he not yielding to a feeling of impotence or of sexual inferiority? Since his ideal is an infinite virility, is there not a phenomenon of diminution in relation to the Negro, who is viewed as a penis symbol? Is the lynching of the Negro not a sexual revenge (pp. 122-123)? Also see note 22.

human level" but in different ways. For Fanon, the implication is that the 'whiteman' has an a priori sense of "helplessness" (à la Altman) or Lacanian "fragmentation" and equates its negation with the reaching of a "human level" of mastery, agency and the need for superiority. This is interesting because I believe that there is an underlying existential angst where the 'whiteman' does not intrinsically (in an a priori sense) consider 'himself' human at all[24]. On the other hand, the 'blackman' is already self-constituted as a dialectic to the 'whiteman', so in effect suffers no existential crisis of *being*, just a crisis of *agency*[25]. For me, the Master/Slave dialectic is played out here because as Hegel's slave gains self-affirmation from his work, the 'blackman' is similarly self-affirmed as a dialectical opposite of the 'whiteman', whom he aspires to become. Interestingly, *becoming* 'white' (free) could be an apt description of the 'blackman's' work, where this performative and transformative action is the fundamental root of self-affirmation for the 'whiteman'. Fanon's 'whiteman', on the other hand, shares his existential crisis with Hegel's Master because the 'whiteman' fears that his a priori existence of "self" is a nothingness (not human/fragmented) without the distinction given to him by the 'blackman'[26]. However, I would go one step further and suggest that the 'whiteman' *fears returning* to "nothingness" or fragmentation (castration) so holds on ever more tenaciously to the 'blackman' for his psychic survival.

### *The Tenacity of 'Whiteness'?*

To further explain why racism holds on to its "unique endowments" so doggedly, we can perhaps turn to Judith Butler [74] who talks about how the subject is hailed into being by power whilst internalising and transforming its performative effects. This is a discursive view of the subject, which keeps its

---

[24] Or in other words, the "helplessness" felt by the 'whiteman' comes from a fear of non-existence (an undistinguished/fragmented/castrated "self").

[25] In other words the 'blackman' only began to feel 'black' when the 'whiteman's need to feel white (and human) was initiated by the 'whiteman'. The 'blackman' for himself had always existed in terms of his own agency and "self" (both forming a sense of "humanity") but in the process of colonisation he only lost his agency not his sense of "self" upon becoming 'black'. Hence the 'blackman's struggle with his "double consciousness" and the psychic violence felt by the him as he is inscribed as a 'phobic object': "Mama, see the Negro! I'm frightened!" (p. 84). So Fanon's 'blackman' in wanting to be 'white' is only really wanting a return of his agency NOT his sense of "self" (that was never taken away). The 'whiteman' in performing his agency over the 'blackman' is actually seeking his sense of (complete, unfragmented) "self", which for him completes his "humanity" (the Lacanian 'imago'). I also read a lingering double-meaning in Fanon's use of the word "slaves", where embedded in the meaning is the 'whiteman' that both enslaves and is enslaved by his "search for mastery".

[26] Correspondingly, Hegel's Master gaining self-affirmation from the works of the slave.

essence in perpetual motion; a blurring of the distinct. If we apply this to male 'whiteness', its implied performative genesis becomes very interesting indeed. In this scenario, male 'whiteness' is hailed into being by male 'blackness' as it transforms and internalises the latter's masculine power as its own, in so doing keeping its sense of distinctiveness in perpetual motion. This seems to me to be slightly different to the Lacanian reading of a subject, where he believes that a subject is actuated by its constant realisation of that which alienates and separates it from the "Other". Although Lacan sees this as the subject as never being fully formed or stable, I tend to read this process of alienation and separation as an additive process where the "self" is constantly growing in self-awareness and it is the subject that houses this growth or movement of the self. In other words, the first process of alienation and separation can be seen as the original identifier of the self where other phases of alienation and separation act to re-enforce and/or "re-articulate" the first process. In this sense, the primary acts of alienation and separation can be viewed as a "line of tendential force" [75] beyond which we cannot meaningfully re-articulate.

However, Butler sees the subject as being even more inherently unstable and unknowable than Lacan, as she posits that even the formation of the "self" is from the outset contaminated by power. Butler assumes that there must exist "a paradox of referentiality" (p.4) where she admits that talking about a subject who takes in power without knowing what constitutes the subject is a paradox because, "our reference continues to make a certain kind of sense" (p.4) and points to a need for a clear a priori "I" distinction of the subject. Instead, Butler contorts the figuration of "I" (in our context, 'whiteness') to a retrospective piece of reflexion based on a theory of "passionate attachment." This is where the subject (which is still unconstituted via the paradox of referentiality) becomes passionately attached to its means of subordination (subjectivation), as it equates its subordination to a prerequisite for its survival - putting 'blackness' and its Hegelian function in a very interesting place. This process of passionate attachment, according to Butler, is both acknowledged and denied by the subject, in so doing forming a retrospective "I" in denying this, (by now) internalised subordination. This very much echoes Neil Altman's theory of 'whiteness' with "'blackness' as its disavowed double." The "I" or in our case 'whiteness', is appalled by the knowledge that it is complicit in its own subordination (c.f. Fanon's "slaves") in order to survive and furthers its desire for survival, which by now is equated to subordination and is now the very thing that threatens the (structural) integrity of the "I." It is the "I"'s ('whiteness'') desires that actually threaten its survival! So, "I" ('whiteness') lives in a perpetual state of denial of and conflict with its desires for its survival. I see this argument as a reconstituted Master/slave dialectic, where Butlerian "dialogue" is added to the Hegelian "stage directions" of the Master/Slave "script."

This parlous state of existence for a retrospectively articulated "I" is only made possible by the paradox of referentiality. Lacan's Mirror stage suffers from the same challenge as Butler's paradox where in order for the child to feel alienated it must have had a sense of self in the first place. Lacan overcomes this by positing that the process of alienation is somehow intrinsic in forming the sense of self whereas Butler continues to explain that there is an "ambivalence" concerning where the power comes from and its adoption by the subject. Butler concludes that "the subject is neither fully determined by power nor fully determining of power (but significantly and partially both)" (p.17). In our context, this is an important point that Butler offers because 'whiteness' can also be seen as neither fully determined by 'blackness' nor fully determining of 'blackness' (but significantly and partially both).

Despite the perpetual motion of 'whiteness' and its constitution, its drive for survival and mastery makes it particularly difficult to overcome in the real world. Perhaps thinking of its drive for survival as "jouissance" might help to explain its unusual tenacity. Lacan [76] talks of a "jouissance" (p. 17) that is loosely translated as "enjoyment/pleasure" but it can have more of a Freudian libidinal connotation, although Lacan has more spiritual connotations in his many usages as the 'ultimate' (my word) drive[27]. Earlier, I conglomerated 'need' and 'want'[28] but in psychoanalytical terms there is a significant difference between the two. I would characterise 'need' as something, which can be satisfied such as hunger and Lacan would (probably) agree. However, for me, 'want' is characterised by the unattainable or the "Lack (of)," which Lacan would recognise as a desire and I suspect Fanon had this in mind with his question. This is important as the "I"'s ('whiteness'') fight for survival can be both described by its needs which are 'permanently temporary', as they are in the constant process of being satisfied and also by their antitheses; desires, which are constantly not being satisfied.

As discussed, this alienation/separation process is shifting and can be described as a "line of tendential force". However, it would appear that the

[27] Where the subject constantly wants to go beyond the 'pleasure principle'; i.e., that which prescribes 'acceptable' levels of pleasure, beyond which pleasure turns into suffering, as the subject can only experience a certain amount of pleasure.

[28] See note 23.

indivisible element that constitutes the 'self' is desire; "the essence of man" (p. 275)[29] [77, 78].

Although Lacan recognises desire to be the "essence" of the subject, its shifting patterns of visiting signifier after signifier can be seen as a series of articulations, as desire is fixed in a perpetual state of desiring (going beyond its pleasure principle).

However, I would tend to view the desire to exceed the 'pleasure principle' as an essential 'ball park' within which to look for the "essence of man" (essence of 'whiteness'). In this 'ball park' of desire, I read Lacan as finally locating the indivisible essence (which cannot be re-articulated à la Hall) as, "jouissance", which is the ultimate form of never having enough (pleasure) which all drives lead to, definitely an all roads leading to Rome concept.

However, for Lacan, what makes "jouissance" ultimate and essential is its position as a quasi-Platonic Ideal in which all other drives find death, their ultimate satisfaction.

Lacan sees this as the defining factor behind the formation of the self. I see this "jouissance" as constituting the self-preservation of the subject preventing it from being totally cannabalised by Power, a sort of living in ('towards') "jouissance" right up to the moment of death, thus somehow imbuing existence with a hyper real vitality that is circumscribed by its impending end thus making the fight for its existence all the more urgent. I have described this "jouissance"-journey towards death as a Freudian death drive.

However, I interpret Lacan as characterising this journey as not really being driven towards death but being driven by death[30] [79]. I read Lacan's nuance as describing a foreknowledge of death and its ultimate satisfaction and this foreknowledge being carried as a present-knowledge driving the superego towards its much-welcomed future satisfaction.

So, if we begin to understand 'whiteness' (and its relationship to its own desires and drives), in terms of its knowing journey towards "jouissance", as it is hailed into existence by its unconscious and undifferentiated needs (i.e., its "terror of human freedom" and fragmentation), its pathology and its persistence begins to make much more sense. The subsequent development of 'whiteness' then becomes a story of how it negotiates/subdues/sublimates its

[29] A reminder that Lacan is very much influenced by Baruch Spinoza's "desire is the essence of man" (p. 128) from his 1677 work, Ethics.

[30] Lacan says that the death drive is actually a component of all drives and not a specific drive in itself.

drives and desires, in so doing constructing the "Other" (i.e., 'blackness') to form a dialectical "I" (us) and "You" (them).

## The Psychopolitics of 'Whiteness' in the Real World

In reading Pankaj Mishra's excellent think piece *How to think about Islamic State* [80], I was struck by his description of globalisation as almost being like a Western virus that is infecting the whole world where, "capital continually moves across national boundaries in the search for profit, contemptuously sweeping skills and norms made obsolete by technology into the dustbin of history."

Mishra locates the "unique endowment" of globalisation as "self-interest." Self-interest, for Mishra is a form of individual agency or mastery. His central thesis is that individuals are promised individual agency within our contemporary neoliberal paradigm.

Although they (think that they) are educated with the means to achieve agency, they end up frustrated by their eventual failure to achieve it because they seem not to be aware of the hidden asymmetric balance between merit and privilege [81]. Mishra describes how the promise of freedom is spread around the world and how the ensuing frustrations felt by the recipients of this promise are expressed in vernacularised rebellions and unrests. Furthermore, Mishra proposes that this rampant global focus on materialism has hollowed out alternative non-material world views such as religion or spirituality, very much echoing Krishnaswarmy's view that "corporate globalization is thriving precisely by emptying out the subversive potential in culture."

However, it is this concept of 'self-interest' that reminds me of mastery within the context of 'whiteness'. As Altman has already noted, the search for mastery becomes a psychopathological structure when it requires a disavowed opposite (to master). It strikes me that in the search for mastery and freedom; we have a conceptual meeting place between globalisation and 'whiteness'. If we accept that neoliberalism is the driving force behind globalisation where individualism is deified, then what we are actually describing is a form of global 'whiteness' where disavowed antitheses are created in order to service the search for (individual) mastery, which manifests itself as *individual* wealth accumulation in market terms. In order to explore this search for mastery and its disavowed antitheses in market terms, I will briefly discuss David Graeber's [82] intriguing argument that Capitalism can be viewed as a transformation of Slavery.

He makes comparisons between the two modes of production by examining one of their common denominators namely, "abstract labour"[31] [83, 84]. Graeber describes "abstract labour" as "pure creative potential. This is created by the effects of command. Abstract labor is the sheer power of creation, to do anything at all." (p. 79). I think this resonates with Morrison's "terror of human freedom" rather well. This is fascinating because, if we

[31] David Graeber makes these five comparisons (pp. 79 – 80):

(1) Both rely on a separation of the place of social (re)production of the labor force, and the place where that labor-power is realized in production – in the case of slavery, this is effected by transporting laborers bought or stolen from one society into another one; in capitalism, by separating the domestic sphere (the sphere of social production) from the workplace. In other words, what is effected by physical distance in one is effected by the anonymity of the market in the other.
(2) The transfer is effected through exchanging human powers for money: either by selling workers, or hiring them (essentially, allowing them to rent themselves).
(3) One effect of that transfer is 'social death', in the sense that the community ties, kinship relations and so forth that shaped the worker are, in principle, supposed to have no relevance in the workplace. This is true in capitalism too, at least in principle: a worker's ethnic identity, social networks, kin ties and the rest should not have any effect on hiring or how one is treated in the office or shop floor, though of course in reality this isn't true.
(4) Most critically, the financial transaction in both cases produces abstract labor, which is pure creative potential. This is created by the effects of command. Abstract labor is the sheer power of creation, to do anything at all. Everyone might be said to control abstract labor in their own person, but in order to extend it further, one has to place others in a position where they will be effectively an extension of one's will, completely at one's orders. Slavery, military service and various forms of corvée are the main forms in which this has manifested itself historically. Obviously, this too is something of an unrealized ideal: this is in fact precisely the area of most labor struggle. But it's worthy of note that feudalism (or manorialism if you prefer) tends towards exactly the opposite principle: the duties owed by liege to lord were very specific and intricately mapped out.
(5) A constant ideological accompaniment of this sort of arrangement is an ideology of freedom. As Moses Finley first pointed out (1980), most societies take it for granted that no human is completely free or completely dependent, rather, all have different degrees of rights and obligations. The modern ideal of political liberty, in fact, has historically tended to emerge from societies with extreme forms of chattel slavery (Pericles' Athens, Jefferson's Virgina), essentially as a point of contrast. Medieval jurists, for example, assumed every right was someone else's obligation and vice versa; the modern doctrine of liberty as a property of humans one could possess was developed precisely in Lisbon and Antwerp, the cities that were at the center of the slave trade at the time; and the most common objection to this new notion of liberty at the time was that if one owns one's freedom, it should then also be possible to sell it (Tuck, 1979). Hence the doctrine of personal liberty – outside the workplace – or even the notion of freedom of contract, that one so often encounters in societies dominated by wage labor, does not really mean we are dealing with a fundamentally different sort of system. It means we are dealing with a transformation. We are dealing with the same terms, differently arranged, so that rather than one class of people being able to imagine themselves as absolutely 'free' because others are absolutely unfree, we have the same individuals moving back and forth between these two positions over the course of the week and working day.

revisit the Lacanian Mirror stage of alienation for 'whiteness' (subject), "abstract labour" could also be cast as one of the prime components of 'blackness' (the disavowed imago). In order to identify and to strive to become the imago, the subject ('whiteness') needs to master (possess) the imago (to master his "terror of human freedom"!) Here we can see that in calling 'blackness' into being as the imago, "the sheer power of creation, to do anything at all" (in other words, abstract labour) was also being hailed into being at the site of alienation. Graeber goes on to describe the performative nature of abstract labour as, "effectively an extension of [another] one's will, completely at [another] one's orders." So here we have a state of affairs where not only is the potential existence of infinite power ("to do anything at all") hailed into being upon alienation (or command through mastery) but also hailed into being is the possibility of its physical manifestation as labour power. The Master/Slave dialectic would appear to lie at the heart of the capitalist programme and therefore its ensuing globalisation because in order to exist, the Master has to depend on the labour power of his slave. However, more profoundly, the Master's existence is actually derived from the "abstract labour" of the Slave – symbolising Morrison's "terror of human freedom." So it is the "sheer power of creation" that hails the Master into being in the first place but this potential for creation is located in the site of the Slave and in the commanding of the Slave, the potential for creation (abstract labour) is made physical as (waged) labour power and the Master is then created. Crucially, the Master accumulates wealth or capital by paying a wage for labour power, which is less than the value of its abstract counterpart – so, in effect, the worker constantly produces more than for what they are actually paid (this produces a surplus or profit). This is important because it is the profit that creates the mastery, without the profit, this would become a mere "exchange" between equals (on a like for like basis). In fact, I would suggest that the Master is only fully constituted through the creation of profit, so embedded within abstract labour is the potential for profit, which is the hailing into being of the Master. However, if we also remember that the Slave is validated only by his works not by his Master, we can begin to see the Slave as being free in two fundamental senses. Firstly, the Slave originally free, constructed as abstract labour (and potential profit), represents the "terror of human freedom" (an existential crisis of 'whiteness'). Secondly, the Slave's continued existence is not dependent on the Master but on his (own) works (the potential "to do anything at all" i.e., human freedom). So the Slave remains free throughout the whole process of subjectivation. If we apply Butler's caveat that, "the subject is neither fully determined by power nor fully determining of power (but significantly and partially both)" (p.17) as well as its transposition to/from the whiteness/blackness dialectic, we can, perhaps begin to understand how and why the Master's "passionate attachment" to his Slave manifests itself in the rampant individualism of Capitalism.

### *The Fantasy of 'Individuality' As a Market Derivative of The Fantasy of 'Whiteness'*

Here, I am deliberately alluding to the nature of a market derivative as a contract that gains its value from the performance of an underlying entity of some sort[32] [85]. In the context of this chapter, I will use the idea of the derivative figuratively to cast the fantasy of 'individuality' as a market contract that derives its value from the underlying market performance of the fantasy of 'whiteness'[33]. This contract is brokered by the market and is between the social being and Afro Neo Romanticism. I will unpack the significance of this, as I explain how (hidden) social knowledge, re-packaged as 'individuality' is traded through goods and services and more specifically how it is underpinned by 'whiteness', as it trades as a market derivative (a tool of obscuration). Massimo De Angelis [86] gives us clues as to how the Master's ('whiteness'') "passionate attachment" remains hidden or invisible and how this is achieved by creating the illusion of "individuality." To explain this, De Angelis uses Friedrich Hayek's [87, 88] and Jeremy Bentham's [89, 90] models of market coordination as examples. For Hayek (p. 25)

> The sum of the knowledge of all the individuals exists nowhere as an integrated whole. The great problem is how we can all profit from this knowledge, which exists only dispersed as the separate, partial, and sometimes conflicting beliefs of all men.

Hayek is implying here that the system is just too large and complex to be knowable by a single entity (an individual or corporate entity). Hayek says that individuals are in command of much more knowledge than they can articulate because this knowledge is embedded in the goods and services that they use – he calls this tacit knowledge. If we accept that market transactions are actually a form of social transaction where it is knowledge that is being transacted

[32] Rene M. Stulz (p. 4) gives a thorough breakdown of the complexities of derivatives and their market uses. Perhaps the most straightforward example of such a contract is a Forward where it "obligates one party to buy the underlying [asset] at a fixed price at a certain time in the future, called "maturity", from a counterparty who is obligated to sell the underlying at that fixed price."

[33] Later, I will briefly apply the Equity Swap, another type of derivative to demonstrate this.

through the product [91], this idea becomes interesting on a number of fronts. It is this embedded knowledge that Hayek regards as 'social knowledge'. According to Hayek each individual although in command of their 'tacit knowledge' cannot properly capitalise on this knowledge because they are unable to see the whole picture of how their pieces of social knowledge fit together to form a (hypothetical) whole. Hayek suggests that the market mechanism thrives on the individual's incomplete social knowledge (i.e., via their dispersal and isolation as individuals, creating potential conflicts of interests due to the individuals' plans not fitting together in the market-field). By offering opportunities to the individual that appear to benefit them (i.e., providing clues in the form of market prices and other indicators about the embedded social knowledge and social interaction) the market via the potential market conflicts of interests born out of an incomplete social knowledge, is able to make a profit. Here, Hayek's premise of the *individual* needs to be examined, as it is almost taken as an independently a priori facet of market existence. Instead of looking at the individual as a pre-formed non-social entity that enters the market, it might be more useful to see the individual as a *social being* made performatively into an *individual* by the market. Graeber maintains that the social being, upon entering the market, falls victim to the, "*separation of the place of social (re)production of the labor force, and the place where that labor-power is realized in production*" (p. 79, original italics). For Graeber, this makes "social death," in the sense that the community ties, kinship relations and so forth that shaped the worker are, in principle, supposed to have no relevance in the workplace." (p. 79) It would appear that the (continued) freedom of "Slave" is kept from the social being by their individualisation (thanks to their "social death" in the market-field) and the mechanism used to hide the social being's freedom is the fantasy of "individuality"[34] [92-94]. Since "individuality" is presented as a mechanism of

[34] The psychologist, Paul Verhaeghe describes how our psyches have been shaped by neoliberal 'choice' where in fact we have very little choice but to be corralled into following very specific neoliberal ideologies that favour specific character traits (e.g., risk taking, bullying, lying etc.) over others. Verhaeghe quotes the Polish sociologist Zygmunt Bauman as observing, that "[n]ever have we been so free. Never have we felt so powerless." This very much reminds me of Toni Morrison's observations about the early European settlers who were faced with the "terror of human freedom". However, our current 'terror of human freedom' would now seem to be only a Baudrillardian fourth level simulation of freedom which bears no relation to actual freedom (because it is actually a form of control) but nevertheless has the power to invent its own provenance and verisimilitude. This would very much correspond to a post-modern cultural memory enabled by its use of mass communication technologies à la Pierre Nora. See Chapter 2 about the international myth of freedom and democracy.

liberation to achieve individual market freedom[35] [95-97], it is ironic that in reality individualism is actually only operating as a tool of control that attempts to erase the memory of the *continuing* state of the social being's freedom (connectedness, meaning their *interconnected* plans!) through obscuration if not through actual enslavement. It is here that Huck's fantasy of 'whiteness' (freedom) derived in opposition to Jim's supposed 'blackness' (enslavement) is brought to mind – the individual *remains* a social being (with interconnected plans) within the market even if only *tacitly* (i.e., the social being's continued freedom is *not* dependent on their market individualisation)[36]. Seen in this light, the market is not a neutral, passive, mechanical entity merely coordinating pre-packaged individuals with no social history. The market is an active, conscious network of social interactions with the power to reshape the social being into an individual for its own biases (i.e., profit) [98]. The market can only do this if it has the powers of a cultural institution, which is how I describe the market, elsewhere [99]. The market is cultural in the sense of generating a consensus through its social networks to reduce the social being to an individual whilst using the stripped away social knowledge of the individual to determine market prices (its combined cultural aims). The market is an institution because it assumes a mix of Foucauldian and Bourdieusian powers to enact its cultural aims through the 'negotiation' of property rights. So, in Hayek, we have a situation where the market (Master) is trying to obscure its passionate attachment (its reliance on) to the social being-cum-individual (Slave). Lacan would perhaps characterise this process of

[35] Which according to Richard Tuck is a commodity that is owned not a state of being meaning that it can be legally sold (or taken away).

[36] This is interesting because Graeber implies that the market has the power to inflict 'social death' on the now individual, especially by the separation of the social reproduction of the labour force and the site where the labour power is realised. Here I would argue that although the market might have the strong intention to do this and achieves this to a degree, it is only ever partial because the imprint of the social ties and relationships remains embedded in the very social knowledge that is being transacted. In a way what I am saying is that the "unique endowment" of social knowledge and relationships as (partially) expressed through goods and services remains dictating its terms of affiliation from afar like, Edward Said's "attitudes of a dominating metropolitan center ruling a distant territory". Indeed, it is this very "unique endowment" that is used by the market to secretly assign value to a transacted social knowledge or divest it of its value. Even in the extreme case of African chattel slavery, people were literally taken from one geographical location to another. This separated the social reproduction of labour from its physical manifestation, the 'social death' inflicted on them through broken kinship ties was only ever partial because an imprint (a yearning, a recollection, a re-imagination) of those ties lived on and shaped the new social formations that were produced in the creolised aftermath of the forced re-location.

separation as repression where the market is repressing its awareness of its own lack (castration) in regards to its relationship to the 'individual'[37].

Jeremy Bentham's *Panopticon: or the Inspection-House* [100], perhaps illustrates this form of market repression more clearly. Bentham's panopticon consists of separate cells arranged in a circle overlooking a central courtyard with a watch tower in the middle. Each of the cells contains an individual. The watch tower contains an inspector who is keeping a watch on all of the surrounding cells. Each cell houses an individual whose plans are unclear to the inspector. All the inspector knows is that each individual in their separate cells is held captive and wants to escape and this desire for freedom means that they do not complete all of the tasks required of them by the inspector. So the inspector has to keep watch over all of them to make sure that they do the work required. However the occupants of each cell cannot see into the courtyard which means that they cannot see the inspector. The inspector on the other hand can see into their cells via some sort of illuninated translucent screen (Indonesian shadow puppetry comes to mind) but can only make out the shadows of the occupants so is unsure of the precise nature of their actions (just the *effect* of their actions as they cast shadows on the screen). Bentham describes this as, "the *centrality* of the inspector's situation, combined with the well known and most effectual contrivances for *seeing without being seen*" (p. 21).

The cell-occupants cannot see if they are being inspected at any given moment and in fact the inspector cannot surveil *all* the cell-occupants at *all* times. In order to maintain control, the inspector has to make the cell-occupants *believe* that they are being surveilled constantly, which s/he is successful in doing by exacting rewards or punishments depending on how well the tasks are executed.

One of the striking points of Bentham's panopticon model of the market is the opacity between the inspector and the (cell-)occupant. For me, this is intriguing because the inspector is not aware of the occupants' plans and s/he

[37] Interestingly in following Lacan's script for the separation process, the Phallus or jouissance is representative of the social ties/knowledge of the social being. The market realises that it itself does not have the social ties (knowledge) of the social being (the Phallus/jouissance). It therefore suffers symbolic castration but in a twist to the script, instead of merely realising (recognising) the lack of Phallus in the Mother and as a result her symbolic castration, the Mother who in our case represents the social being, prior to entering the market does possess the Phallus. So the market attempts to castrate the social being of its Phallus in order to reshape it into an "individual", whilst seeking the Phallus/jouissance for itself, as represented by the market trying to use the "individual's" social ties and knowledge for its own ends as represented by prices and other market indicators to assign or divest market value (c.f. N'yong'o's "Participation as Neoliberal Fantasy").

also cannot be truly certain whether the occupant is really isolated from their (next door) neighbour. This is significant because what the inspector does know is that the occupants desire freedom from their cell and sabotage their tasks but what the inspector cannot know is whether these sabotaged tasks are coordinated or not. Hayek makes the assumption that the individuals' plans are uncoordinated in the market but Bentham's model is not quite so certain. If we remember that the inspector can only see shadowy impressions of the occupants against the screen, this means that at the very best, the inspector can only guess at what the occupants' real activities are. If we transpose this model to social knowledge, it is clear that the inspector has no real access to the social knowledge (or the potential social connectedness) of the occupant so s/he can only use the shadows to act as estimated valuations of the occupant's social knowledge.

At the same time, the occupant cannot see the inspector but is made to believe via the rewards and punishments they receive that the inspector is watching them constantly. It is obviously no coincidence that Michel Foucault in his *Discipline and Punish* [101] was interested in this manner of mind control or *discipline power* because in order for Bentham's inspector to maintain control (as in to keep on extracting labour through the tasks), s/he has to convince the occupants of their omnipresence or more precisely their 'ever watchfulness'[38]. The only way in which the inspector can do that is to encourage the occupants to self-surveil without their being aware, where the rewards and punishments become synonymous with the inspector themselves (or become proxies for the inspector, even where the occupants begin to punish themselves in anticipation of the proxy!) Bentham's model clearly configures the panopticon as an institution with coercive (persuasive) discipline powers from which the occupants want to escape. However, rather intriguingly the inspector can only contrive the rewards or punishments based on their shadow-approximations. So in turn, the market can only reward or penalise the (reluctant) 'individual' based on its approximations of social knowledge, which like abstract labour cannot be fully costed and so will always be costed downwards; this is what we recognise as market costs and other market indicators.

So, both Hayek's and Bentham's models of market coordination cast the social being as an individual although Bentham's model does leave room for doubt. However, the obscuration of the Master's passionate attachment is

[38] This is a slightly different point to the inspector simulating omnipresence because from the perspective of the occupant, the inspector is only ever present to them at any given moment, if the occupant truly has no knowledge of the other occupants.

present in both models because the social being is isolated and cut off to form an individual and also particularly in the panopticon, the existence of the inspector and the true nature of the limits of his/her powers is obscured by a one way translucent screen. But the screen also functions as a form of repression (becoming a literal separation (of desires) between the inspector and occupant). The screen represents the inspector's unwillingness to acknowledge that s/he cannot see directly into the cell. So s/he cannot truly ascertain the social knowledge (or cannot acquire the Phallus) being enacted but has to make do with the shadows, convincing themselves that there is in fact, no lack of knowledge on their part that the shadows *are* the social knowledge (meaning that they do have the Phallus, after all).

Still exploring the panopticon, the idea that the punishments and rewards become proxies for the inspector from the occupant's point of view, leads us rather usefully to thinking about derivatives. The market can only seem to make its decisions based on approximations or guesses about (the shadows of) the social knowledge that is being traded (and it is those guesses that act as market proxies from the individual's point of view). In order to make the best estimates that it can about the social knowledge (to which it has no direct access and belongs to the social being), it has to institute certain controls that limit the 'unknowable-ness' of this social knowledge. The easiest way to do this is to treat the social being upon entering the market as an individual with partial (or no) social knowledge and *no* knowledge of other social beings' plans. In this way the market is confident that it will be able to make near guesses of these partial packets of social knowledge brought into the market by the now individual. If we apply the concept of the market derivative to 'whiteness' and 'individuality' we might be able to re-fashion Max Horkheimer and Theodor Adorno's [102] views on the cultural industry into the market-oriented Afro Neo Romanticism:

> Anyone who does not conform is condemned to an economic impotence which is prolonged in the intellectual powerlessness of the eccentric loner. Disconnected from the mainstream he is easily convicted of inadequacy (p. 106).

Their prescient thoughts outline how a market commodification of culture is used to pacify the social being into a passive consumer of controlling and manipulative commodified cultural products. Afro Neo Romanticism is a twenty first century update on this idea where an abstracted 'black culture' (an artefact of 'whiteness' c.f. Frantz Fanon) is used as a soft form of globalisation to lay the foundations for (hard) global Americocentrism[39] [103, 104]. Taking my cue from Horkheimer and Adorno, the social being feels that they have to reluctantly enter the cultural market (mainstream) for fear of "social death" (a market tool of coercion). However, in order to successfully enter the (cultural) market they are convinced by the market that the market is the place where they can attain 'true' freedom in the form of an 'individuality' that will enable Simmelian personal re-invention (leading to wealth). However, as discussed they are unaware of the lack of choices being offered to them[40] [105, 106]. In this market scenario, Afro Neo Romanticism (ANR) is the broker. It presents

---

[39] See chapter 2. Steven W Thrasher describes hard global Americocentrism as a "War Machine" that "is the violent nexus of military and economic forces that grinds us up to perpetuate itself." Thrasher outlines how the US' overseas militarianism has been transported inwards and is being used in civil settings predominantly against people of colour in the US. He describes how this hard tool of global power has transformed itself into a 'soft' but nevertheless dangerous influence capable of using cultural products (markets) as tools of social control (reminding me of Louis Althusser's *Ideology and Ideological State Apparatuses*) where:

> The War Machine does not want us as a society to ask of ourselves the difficult questions about why it is that black people, abroad and at home, have been kept in the margins and away from economic opportunity, employment, education and safety. It prefers that we maintain the status quo and uncritically support the state, no matter how violent and oppressive.

Thrasher also characterises the War Machine as a function of 'whiteness' that:

> ...has always had an insatiable need for bodies of color from before the birth of this nation. The genocide of Native Americans, the Atlantic Slave trade of Africans, the conquest of Mexicans, the colonization of Filipinos and Hawaiians, the mass importation of Chinese workers subsequently denied citizenship under the Chinese Exclusion Act: the War Machine created and then expanded the size of the United States using non-white bodies, waging war against them, and making them second-class citizens (when it deigned to make them citizens at all).

[40] 'Individuality' in this context can be represented by the aspiration of property ownership and its accompanying accumulation of wealth. Gary A Dymski gives a great account of how mortgage lenders in the US have historically narrowed the market borrowing choices of African Americans by denying them access to affordable borrowing. Dymski also reports how the lenders sometimes offered them unaffordable borrowing at higher interest rates than their white counterparts in order to precipitate the foreclosure of their properties and perpetuate the narrative of their being high risk borrowers. This practice was commonly known as redlining, as predominantly black neighbourhoods since the 1930s were given a red rating of being high risk borrowers by government agencies such as the Home Owner's Loan Corporation and the Federal Housing Administration. Yves Zenou & Nicolas Boccard also identify the contemporary remnants of the (now illegal) redlining practice as an interplay between racial and spatial discrimination. They say that employers (still) discriminate against people living near the city centre (the so called 'bad areas'), who due to their (on average) lower levels of per capita income have to rely more on public transport to commute to potential work.

cultural products that promise market 'freedoms' (economic, cultural, status etc. wealths). However, in order to trade the cultural product it requires the use of a derivative, in this case an equity swap. An equity swap is a financial derivative where two parties agree to exchange their cash flows for a certain period of time[41]. In our scenario, the agreed exchange is between the social being and ANR, they have agreed to exchange their social knowledge and their market knowledge for a set period decided by the nature of the cultural product.

The social being agrees to pay ANR a fixed rate of interest on its social knowledge. This payment takes the form of "social freedoms," so in effect the social being is giving away its social freedoms to ANR. During this time, the social being becomes an 'individual' in the eyes of the market. ANR at the same time agrees to pay the social being a variable rate of interest on its market knowledge. This takes the form of "individuality," so in effect the market is paying the social being "individuality." However, unknown to the social being at the start of the swap, the "individuality" they are getting paid from ANR is actually a derivative of "whiteness" (masquerading as market knowledge) that is pegged to its performance in the market. At the end of the contractual term, the individual realises that ANR's investment (i.e., 'whiteness-cum-market knowledge) from which their payments of "individuality" comes, has not performed well in the market[42] and has made a

[41] Their cashflows are called legs and one of them is usually pegged to a floating rate such as LIBOR (floating leg), the other pegged to performance of a share or stock (equity leg). Rene Stulz (p. 6) explains the mechanism of a swap like this:

> Suppose that you have an adjustable-rate mortgage with principal of $200,000 and current payments of $10,000 per year. If interest rates double, your payments would increase dramatically. You could eliminate this risk by refinancing your mortgage and getting a fixed-rate mortgage, but the transactions costs could be high. A swap contract would be an alternative solution that would not entail renegotiating the mortgage contract. You would agree to make payments to a counterparty, say a bank, equal to a fixed interest rate applied to $200,000. In exchange, the bank would pay you a floating rate applied to $200,000. With this interest rate swap, you would use the floating-rate payments received from the bank to make your mortgage payments. The only payments you would make out of your own pocket would be the fixed interest payments to the bank, as if you had a fixed-rate mortgage. Therefore, a doubling of interest rates would no longer affect your mortgage payments.

[42] In reality, this would not be surprising, as the market is only using guesstimates of the social knowledge it gained from the social being in the swap in order to make its decisions – its guesstimates acting as floating interest rates (that can go up or down). In fact, the market's stock is totally dependent on the 'individual's' market performance of 'whiteness' (unbeknown to the individual). Its stock comprises an aggregate of 'individual' market performances of 'whiteness'.

loss. ANR as part of the contract has to give its losses to the individual (as it would, its profits). In reality, this means that the individual has to pay ANR the value of its losses[43].

This analogy attempts to show in market terms how the social being is duped into entering the market in exchange for a market simulation of freedom but all the while through a commoditised cultural product, they are being wrought as a disavowed (or repressed) antithesis to 'whiteness' (or proximity to 'whiteness'[44] [107, 108]).

## CONCLUSION

In this chapter, I have explored how the "unique endowment" of globalisation is in fact 'whiteness' in its marketised form of "individuality" and using a psychoanalytical lens, I have attempted to uncover its pathologically tenacious grip on the psyche of the marketised 'individual'. I have purposely expressed 'whiteness' as an expanded market construct of Afro Neo Romanticism in order to illustrate how the market (globally) *homogenises* (or hegemonises) the social being into 'whiteness' or proximities to 'whiteness' through its individualising market mechanisms. In other words, I have discussed how the market assigns or divests value depending on the 'individual's' market performance of 'whiteness', the results of which are

[43] In the real world, meaning paying the price for engaging in ANR as a consumer (i.e., trading in 'whiteness') and being negatively branded by the approximations of (hidden) social knowledge ('whiteness') used to divest the individual of market (and social) value (in the form of stereotyping, cultural racism, institutional racism etc. See Chapter 2). Of course, not all market 'individuals' make a loss in this equity swap!

[44] Nashwa Khan gives a great account of how the globalised nature of 'whiteness' has manifested itself in the contemporary portrayal of South Asian women in US sitcoms. Khan argues that the central South Asian character, Mindy Lahiri who is a doctor, in the Mindy Project and who in assuming 'whiteness' or a "proximity to whiteness" creates an antithetical 'blackness' from the African American character called Tamra Webb who is the show's (only black) practice nurse. Khan examines, what she calls, the "anti-black" humour of the show that stereotypes African Americans as "ghetto" and unintelligent in order to emphasise the South Asian's (aspirational) "proximity to whiteness" where "only the Indian woman and her white cast are expected to be reasonable and intellectual." This is a strong example of how a marketised 'whiteness'/'blackness' dialectic is played out in the cultural industry (market), where the "unique endowment" of this narrative no longer refers to specific ethnic markers but to a generic mode of market relationships that are framed by the (market) performance of 'whiteness'. Also see Chapter 2 for an example of how anti-blackness within the 'proximity to whiteness' discourse led to a fatal stabbing of a Nigerian teacher by a Pakistani pupil in the northern town of Bradford in the UK.

manifested globally in *heterogeneous* surface forms of 'resistance' peculiar to their vernacular environments.

## Epilogue

In thinking about the very real consequences of 'whiteness' in everyday life and how this can be resisted, I was touched by Erika Kleinman's [109] very honest piece, *You Don't Have to Be Racist to Benefit From White Privilege*, where in echoing Peggy McIntosh [110], she suggests reflection and reflexivity in developing a personal awareness of this phenomenon:

> If there was one small way for white progressives to educate themselves, what would that look like? Read about white privilege and white fragility and how it works, particularly how to unpack it. Read books by black authors: James Baldwin, Ta-Nehisi Coates, Toni Morrison. Listen to the interview on This Week in Blackness (TWIB) with Marissa Janae Johnson.
>
> Intentionally put yourself in situations where you'll be around more people of color, including prioritizing diversity when choosing your child's school. Listen to people of color and resist the urge to defend your ego. Be willing to be humble, imperfect. Have real conversations with your kids about race, even if it's awkward for both of you. Get better at it. Join groups agitating for racial justice.

Elsewhere [111], I write about how communities have historically organised protests and movements that register their resistance to the concomitant effects of 'whiteness' and globalisation but as Kleinman points out, those who unwittingly benefit from this system also need to resist it, if movements like #BlackLivesMatters are to have any lasting effects for all of us.

## REFERENCES

[1] Clennon, O. (2015). Urban Dialectics, The Market and Youth Engagement: The 'Black' Face of Eurocentrism. New York: Nova Science Publishers.

[2] Krishnaswarmy, R. (2002). The criticism of culture and the culture of criticism at the intersection of postcolonialism and globalisation theory. *Diacritics*, 32(2), 106 - 126.

[3] Benjamin, W. (1999). The Arcades Project. (R. Tiedemann, Ed., H. Eiland, and K. McLaughlin, Trans.) Cambridge MA: Harvard University Press.

[4] Said, E. (1983). Traveling Theory. In E. Said, The World, The Text, The Critic (pp. 226-247). Cambridge, MA: Harvard University Press.

[5] Appadurai, A. (1996). Modernity At Large: Cultural Dimensions of Globalization. Minneapolis, MN: University of Minnesota Press.

[6] García Canclini, N. (1989). Hybrid Cultures: Strategies for Entering and Leaving Modernity. (C. L. Chiappari, and S. L. Lopez, Trans.) Minneapolis: University of Minnesota.

[7] Robertson, R. (1992). Globalization: Social Theory and Global Culture. London: Sage.

[8] Featherstone, M. (1990). Global Culture: An introduction. In M. Featherstone (Ed.), Global Culture: Nationalism, Globalization and Modernity (pp. 1 - 14). London: Sage.

[9] Tomlinson, J. (1999). Globalization and Culture. Chicago: University of Chicago Press.

[10] Jameson, F. (1998). Notes on Globalization as a Philosophical Issue. In F. Jameson, and M. Miyoshi (Eds.), The Cultures of Globalisation (pp. 54 - 80). Durham, NC: Duke University Press.

[11] Jameson, F. (1984). Postmodernism; or, The Cultural Logic of Late Capitalism. *New Left Review,* 146(July - August), 59 - 92.

[12] Waters, M. (1995). Globalization. New York: Routledge.

[13] Hall, S. (2000). Conclusion: The Multi-cultural Question. In B. Hesse (Ed.), Un/settled Multiculturalisms: Diasporas, Entanglemnts, Transruptions (pp. 209 - 241). London: Zed Books.

[14] Schiller, H. I. (1976). Communication and Cultural Domination. White Plains, NY: International Arts and Sciences Press.

[15] Radhakrishnan, R. (2001). Globalization, Desire and the Politics of Representation. *Comparative Literature*, 53(4), 315 - 332.

[16] Ashcroft, B., Griffiths, G., and Tiffen, H. (1998). Key Concepts in Post-Colonial Studies. London: Routledge.

[17] Clennon, O. (2015). Urban Dialectics, The Market and Youth Engagement: The 'Black' Face of Eurocentrism. New York: Nova Science Publishers.

[18] Benjamin, W. (1999). The Arcades Project. (R. Tiedemann, Ed., H. Eiland, and K. McLaughlin, Trans.) Cambridge MA: Harvard University Press.
[19] Appadurai, A. (1996). Modernity At Large: Cultural Dimensions of Globalization. Minneapolis, MN: University of Minnesota Press.
[20] Jay, P. (2001). Beyond Discipline? Globalisation and the Future of English. *PMLA,* 116(1), 32 - 47.
[21] Nyong'o, T. (2012). Queer Africa and the Fantasy of Virtual Participation. *WSQ: Women's Studies Quarterly*, 40(1-2), 40 - 63.
[22] Robertson, R. (1995). Glocalization: Time-Space and Homogeneity-Heterogneity. In M. Featherstone, S. Lash, and R. Robertson (Eds.), Global Modernities (pp. 25 - 44). London: Sage.
[23] Swyngedouw, E. (2004). Globalisation or 'Glocalisation'? Networks, Territories and Rescaling. *Cambrige Review of International Affairs,* 17(1), 25 - 48.
[24] Krishnaswarmy, R. (2002). The criticism of culture and the culture of criticism at the intersection of postcolonialism and globalisation theory. *Diacritics*, 32(2), 106 - 126.
[25] Massey, D. (1994). Space, Place and Gender. Minneapolis: University of Minnesota Press.
[26] Jreisat, J. E. (2009). Administration, Globalization and the Arab States. *Public Organizationl Review*, 9, 37 - 50.
[27] Kirk, D., Cooke, C., Flintoff, A., and McKenna, J. (2008). Key concepts in sport and exercise. London: Sage.
[28] Said, E. (1983). Traveling Theory. In E. Said, The World, The Text, The Critic (pp. 226-247). Cambridge, MA: Harvard UP.
[29] Said, E. (1994). Culture and Imperialism. New York: Vintage Books.
[30] St Louis, B. (2007). Rethinking Race, Politics, and Poetics: C.L.R. James' Critique of Modernity. Routledge: New York and Abingdon.
[31] Appadurai, A. (1996). Modernity At Large: Cultural Dimensions of Globalization. Minneapolis, MN: University of Minnesota Press.
[32] Dusche, M. (2014). Women's Rights in India: Hierarchical Ethics vs. Egalitarian Morality. *South Asia Chronicle*, 4, 228 - 253.
[33] Hall, S. (2000). Conclusion: The Multi-cultural Question. In B. Hesse (Ed.), Un/settled Multiculturalisms: Diasporas, Entanglemnts, Transruptions (pp. 209 - 241). London: Zed Books.
[34] Butler, J. (1997). The Psychic Life of Power. Stanford: Stanford University Press.

[35] Foucault, M. (1977). Discipline and Punish: The Birth of the Prison. (A. Sheridan, Trans.) New York: Random House.
[36] Clennon, O. (2015). Urban Dialectics, The Market and Youth Engagement: The 'Black' Face of Eurocentrism. New York: Nova Science Publishers.
[37] Nas (Composer). (1994). Illmatic. [Nas, Performer] [CD]. New York: Columbia Records.
[38] Dyson, M. E., and Daulatzai, S. (Eds.). (2010). Born To Use Mics: Reading Nas's Illmatic. New York: Basic Civitas Books.
[39] Noble, D. (2012). Born to use Mics: A book review. *The Journal of Pan African Studies,* 4(9), 164 - 169.
[40] Clennon, O. (2015). Urban Dialectics, The Market and Youth Engagement: The 'Black' Face of Eurocentrism. New York: Nova Science Publishers.
[41] Kvifte, T. (2001). Hunting for the Gold at the end of the Rainbow: Identity and Global Romanticism On the Roots of Ethnic Music. Retrieved July 26, 2013, from Popular Musicology Online: http://www.popular-musicology-online.com/issues/04/kvifte.html
[42] Marshall, E., Staples, J., and Gibson, S. (2009). Ghetto Fabulous: Reading Black Adolescent Femininity in Contemporary Urban Street Fiction. *Journal of Adolescent and Adult Literacy*, 53(1), 28-36.
[43] Du Bois, W. (1935 [1998]). Black Reconstruction in America 1860 - 1880. New York: The Free Press.
[44] Aretha, D. (2013). Awesome African-American Rock and Soul Musicians. Berkeley Heights, NJ: Enslow Publishers.
[45] Bulhan, H. A. (1985). Franz Fanon and the psychology of oppression. New York and London: Plenum Press.
[46] Hook, D. (2005). A critical psychology of the postcolonial. *Theory and Psychology,* 15(4), 475 - 503.
[47] Fanon, F. (1963). The Wretched of the Earth. (C. Farrington, Trans.) New York: Grove Press.
[48] Fanon, F. (1986[1952]). Black Skin, White Masks. (C. L. Markmann, Trans.) London: Pluto Press.
[49] Biko, S. B. (1978). I write what I like. London: Bowerdean Press.
[50] Biko, S. B. (2003). Black Consciousness and the quest for a true humanity. In P. H. Coetzee, and A. P. Roux (Eds.), The African Philosophy Reader: A Text with Readings (Second ed., pp. 79 - 85). London: Routledge.

[51] Morrison, T. (1993). Playing in the Dark: Whiteness and the Literary. New York: Vintage.
[52] Mudimbe, V. (1988). The Invention of Africa. Gnosis, Philosophy and the Order of Knowledge. Bloomington: Indiana University Press.
[53] Hegel, G. (1977). The Phenomenology of Spirit. (A. V. Miller, Trans.) Oxford: Clarendon Press.
[54] Twain, M. (1884). The Adventures of Huckleberry Finn. New York: Penguin.
[55] Altman, N. (2006). Whiteness. *The Psychoanalytic Quarterly*, LXXV(1), 45 - 72.
[56] Clennon, O. (2015). Urban Dialectics, The Market and Youth Engagement: The 'Black' Face of Eurocentrism. New York: Nova Science Publishers.
[57] Patterson, M., and Elliott, R. (2002). Negotiating masculinities: Advertising and the inversion of the male gaze. *Consumption Markets and Culture,* 5(3), 231 - 46.
[58] Collins, P. H. (2000). Black Feminist Thought: Knowledge, Consciousness and the Politics of Empowerment (Second ed.). London: Routledge.
[59] Fanon, F. (1986 [1952]). Black Skin, White Masks. (C. L. Markmann, Trans.) London: Pluto Press.
[60] Clennon, O. (2015). Urban Dialectics, The Market and Youth Engagement: The 'Black' Face of Eurocentrism. New York: Nova Science Publishers.
[61] Collins, P. H. (2004). Black sexual politics: African Americans, gender and the new racism. New York: Routledge.
[62] hooks, b. (2004). We Real Cool: Black Men and Masculinity. London and New York: Routledge.
[63] Jackson, C. (2011). Violence, Visual Culture, and the Black Male Body. New York, Oxford: Routledge.
[64] Jackson, P. (1994). Black male: Advertising and the cultural politics of masculinity. Gender, Place and Culture: *A Journal of Feminist Geography,* 1(1), 49 - 59.
[65] Collins, P. H. (2006). New commodities, new consumers: Selling blackness in a global marketplace. *Ethnicities,* 6(3), 297 – 317.
[66] Vallotton, C. (2011). Babies open our minds to their minds: How "listening" to infant signs complements and extends our knowledge of infants and their development. *Infant Mental Health Journal*, 32(1), 115-133.

[67] Lacan, J. (2006 [2002]). Écrits: The First Complete Edition in English. (B. Fink, H. Fink, and R. Grigg, Trans.) New York: W. W. Norton and Company.

[68] Long, E. (1774). The History of Jamaica (Vol. 2). London: T. Lowndes.

[69] Lacan, J. (2006 [2002]). The Signification of the Phallus. In J. Lacan, Ecrits: The First Complete Edition in English (B. Fink, H. Fink, and R. Grigg, Trans., pp. 575 - 697). New York: W. W. Norton and Company.

[70] Lacan, J. (2006 [2002]). Écrits: The First Complete Edition in English. (B. Fink, H. Fink, and R. Grigg, Trans.) New York: W. W. Norton and Company.

[71] Wells-Barnett, I. B. (2014[1892]). On Lynchings. New York: Dover Publications.

[72] Fanon, F. (1986[1952]). Black Skin, White Masks. (C. L. Markmann, Trans.) London: Pluto Press.

[73] Fanon, F. (1986[1952]). Black Skin, White Masks. (C. L. Markmann, Trans.) London: Pluto Press.

[74] Butler, J. (1997). The Psychic Life of Power. Stanford: Stanford University Press.

[75] Hall, S. (1986). 'On postmodernism and articulation: an interview with Stuart Hall'. (L. Grossberg, Ed.) *Journal of Communication Inquiry,* 10(2).

[76] Lacan, J. (1991). Le Séminaire. Livre XVII. L'envers de la psychanalyse, 1969 - 70. (J. A. Miller, Ed.) Paris: Seuil.

[77] Lacan, J. (1977 [1964]). The Seminar of Jacques Lacan, Book XI: The four fundamental concepts of Psychoanalysis 1964 – 1965. (A. Sheridan, Trans.) London: Hogarth Press and Institute of Psycho-Analysis.

[78] Spinoza, B. (1910[1677]). Ethics. (A. Boyle, Trans.) London: Dent.

[79] Lacan, J. (1977 [1964]). The Seminar of Jacques Lacan, Book XI: The four fundamental concepts of Psychoanalysis 1964 – 1965. (A. Sheridan, Trans.) London: Hogarth Press and Institute of Psycho-Analysis.

[80] Mishra, P. (2015, July 24th). How to think about Islamic State. Retrieved July 28, 2015, from The Guardian: http://www.theguardian.com/books/2015/jul/24/how-to-think-about-islamic-state?CMP=share_btn_tw

[81] Clennon, O. D. (2014, May 21). What's education for, privilege or meritocracy? Retrieved July 28, 2015, from Open democracy: Our Kingdom: https://www.opendemocracy.net/ourkingdom/ornette-clennon/what%E2%80%99s-education-for-privilege-or-meritocracy

[82] Graeber, D. (2006). Turning Modes of Production Inside Out: Or, Why Capitalism is a Transformation of Slavery. *Critique of Anthropology*, 26(1), 61–85.

[83] Finley, M. (1980). Ancient Slavery and Modern Ideology. London: Chatto and Windus.

[84] Tuck, R. (1979). Natural Rights Theories: Their Origin and Development. Cambridge: Cambridge University Press.

[85] Stulz, R. M. (2004). NBER Working Paper Series: Should we fear derivatives? Working Paper 10574. Cambridge, MA: National Bureau of Economic Research. Available at http://www.nber.org/papers/w10574.pdf

[86] De Angelis, M. (2001, May). Global Capital, Abstract Labour, and the Fractal Panopticon. Retrieved August 4, 2015, from The Commoner; Number 1: http://www.commoner.org.uk/fractalpanopt.pdf

[87] Hayek, F. (1960). The Consitution of Liberty. London: Routledge.

[88] Hayek, F. (1976). The Market-order or Catallaxy. In F. Hayek, Law, Legislation and Liberty (Vol. 2, pp. 107-32). London: Routledge and Kegan Paul.

[89] Bentham, J. (1787). Panopticon: or the Inspection-House. Dublin: Thomas Byrne.

[90] Bentham, J. (1824). The book of Fallacies: From Unfinished Papers of Jeremy Hunt. (P. Bingham, Ed.) London: John and H. L. Hunt.

[91] Clennon, O. (2015). Urban Dialectics, The Market and Youth Engagement: The 'Black' Face of Eurocentrism. New York: Nova Science Publishers.

[92] Verhaeghe, P. (2014, September 29). Neoliberalism has brought out the worst in us. Retrieved July 28, 2015, from The Guardian: http://www.theguardian.com/commentisfree/2014/sep/29/neoliberalism-economic-system-ethics-personality-psychopathicsthic

[93] Baudrillard, J. (1981). Simulacra and Simulation. Michigan: University Michigan Press.

[94] Nora, P. (1996). General Introduction: Between Memory and History. In L. D. Krtizmann (Ed.), Realms of Memory: Rethinking the French Past, Vol1: Conflict and Divisions (A. Goldhammer, Trans., pp. 1-20). New York: Columbia University Press.

[95] Tuck, R. (1979). Natural Rights Theories: Their Origin and Development. Cambridge: Cambridge University Press.

[96] Hayek, F. (1960). The Consitution of Liberty. London: Routledge.

[97] Simmel, G. (1971). Georg Simmel: On Individuality and Social Forms. (D. Levine, Ed.) Chicago, IL: University of Chicago Press.
[98] MacKenzie, D., and Millo, Y. (2003). Constructing a Market, Performing Theory: The Historical Sociology of a Financial Derivatives Exchange. *American Journal of Sociology*, 109(1), 107–145.
[99] Clennon, O. (2015). Urban Dialectics, The Market and Youth Engagement: The 'Black' Face of Eurocentrism. New York: Nova Science Publishers.
[100] Bentham, J. (1787). Panopticon: or the Inspection-House. Dublin: Thomas Byrne.
[101] Foucault, M. (1977). Discipline and Punish: The Birth of the Prison. (A. Sheridan, Trans.) New York: Random House.
[102] Horkheimer, M., and Adorno, T. (1944[2002]). Dialectic of Enlightenment: Philosophical Fragments. (G. S. Noerr, Ed., and E. Jephcott, Trans.) London, Stanford, CA: Stanford University Press.
[103] Thrasher, S. W. (2015, January 5). America's War Machine sells fear and loathing beyond Ferguson. Black and brown people pay the price. Retrieved August 9, 2015, from The Guardian: http:// www.theguardian.com/commentisfree/2015/jan/05/america-war-machine-ferguson-nypd-black-people-violence-2015
[104] Althusser, L. (1970). Ideology and Ideological State Apparatuses. Retrieved August 19, 2013, from Marxists.org: http:// www.marxists.org/reference/archive/althusser/1970/ideology.htm
[105] Dymski, G. A. (2006). Discrimination in the credit and housing markets: findings and challenges. In W. M. Rodgers III (Ed.), Handbook on the Economics of Discrimination (pp. 215 - 259). New York: Edward Elgar Publishing.
[106] Zenou, Y., and Boccard, N. (2000). Racial Discrimination and Redlining in Cities. *Journal of Urban Economics*, 48(2), 260–285.
[107] Khan, N. (2015, February 23). "Nope, You Really Can't Say That": My Love/Hate Relationship with The Mindy Project. Retrieved August 8, 2015, from Media Diversified: http://mediadiversified.org/2015/02/23/nope-you-really-cant-say-that-my-lovehate-relationship-with-the-mindy-project/
[108] Kaling, M. (Producer). (2012–15). The Mindy Project [TV Series]. NBC Universal Television Distribution.
[109] Kleinman, E. (2015, August 14). You Don't Have to Be Racist to Benefit From White Privilege. Retrieved August 17, 2015, from Huffington

Post: http://www.huffingtonpost.com/erika-kleinman/the-white-privilege -matri_2_b_7971108.html

[110] McIntosh, P. (1990). White Privilege: Unpacking the Invisible Knapsack. Independent School, Winter, 31-36.

[111] Clennon, O. (2015). Urban Dialectics, The Market and Youth Engagement: The 'Black' Face of Eurocentrism. New York: Nova Science Publishers.

In: International Perspectives of Multiculturalism ISBN: 978-1-63483-971-6
Editor: Ornette D. Clennon 

*Chapter 5*

# CONSIDERING RELATIONAL MULTICULTURALISM: KOREAN ARTISTS' IDENTITY IN TRANSCULTURAL SPACES

***Jeong-Ae Park****
Gongju National University of Education,
South Korea

## ABSTRACT

This chapter presents a review of Jeong-Ae Park's ethnographic research on Korean artists in transcultural spaces. It describes the dynamic processes that shape their identities, which have implications for multicultural education, as they deduce the characteristics of culture. Park's research demonstrates that these artists constitute their new Korean identity in relation to the Other. Through multiple discourses, they are always rediscovering, reinventing, and reinterpreting their Koreanness, as an essential factor of their identity. Based on this understanding of the artists' hybrid identity formation, Park proposes a relational multiculturalism that is concerned with the processes and contexts that construct specific groups' multiple, heterogeneous identities.

* Email: jeong2967@gmail.com

**Keywords:** the third space, liminality, translation, rhizome, multiple hybrid identity, relational multiculturalism

# INTRODUCTION

In the 21st century, more than one hundred and seventy five million people live outside of their native country [1]. Similarly, Korean artists are increasingly choosing to live abroad. The artists' diaspora experience of heterogeneity, diversity and difference provokes a complex, subtle change in their identity. According to Madan Sarup [2], identity formation comprises psychological and sociocultural elements. Furthermore, he explained that an important element of the formation and negotiation of identity is the relation between the past and the present. For Stuart Hall [3], identity is always part narrative and part representation. In other words, one narrates one's identity in one's own self in relation to the Other. Since culture is a group's way of living and surviving, the dynamic identity construction of Korean artists in transcultural spaces is a vital process for conceptualising the characteristic of culture in the globalised world.

Postcolonial theorist Homi K. Bhabha [4] directed attention to "liminal spaces" where a new, usual and (yet) unpredictable hybrid cultural production emerges. For Bhabha, liminal spaces are a "third space" between two original moments in cultural translation. Thus, Bhabha recognised identity as a persistent questioning of the surrounding frames of the space of representation, where the image must confront its difference. What Bhabha termed the third space, I have chosen to call the "transcultural space."

The works of Korean artists abroad simultaneously demonstrate the artists' existing Korean identity and their construction of new Korean identities in constant relation to the Other and a recollected Korea. There is scant research on the phenomenon of hybrid identity-production of diaspora artists' negotiation process with their "cut and mix" (p. 448) [5] of influences. Furthermore, there is little understanding of the process by which artists encounter different cultural factors in order to transform themselves. Therefore, the purpose of the present research was to examine the dynamic processes by which Korean artists shape their identity in the transcultural art world, in order to examine emerging artwork-based hybrid identities. In this chapter I also interpret the meaning and representations of these identities in so doing, exploring the theorisation of multicultural education in the 21st century.

In this chapter, I explore the practical function and effects of the psychic, conceptual and cultural third space that Homi Bhabha theorised. To this end, I interpret my fieldwork with Korean artists who have lived and worked in the international art worlds of New York and London. In particular, I explore how these Korean artists who are active abroad, form a new subjectivity by negotiating contradictory differences between their Koreanness and the Other. Specifically, I examine how artists with Korean roots interact with the differences between the artists and others through their encounters with one another. The questions guiding this inquiry are as follows: How do the Korean artists reconcile their tradition by transforming themselves? How do the artists extend their horizon when they encounter different cultural factors in others? Why do the artists not think that their roots are the only way to bring about new possibilities? And finally, how do they reproduce their roots through their encounters and dialogues with others? To interpret the artists' dynamic formation of their multiple identities, I will also draw on Gilles Deleuze & Félix Guattari's nomadic philosophy in addition to postcolonial theory.

## FIELDWORK WITH KOREAN ARTISTS IN TRANSCULTURAL SPACES

I conducted my fieldwork with Korean artists based in New York in January and August 2010, in March 2011 and in March 2012. During this three-year period, I interviewed thirty seven successful Korean artists in New York. I continued to carry out my fieldwork in London in August and October 2014. Due to changes in the United Kingdom's immigration policy requiring foreign students to leave the country within six months of graduation, the community of London-based Korean artists was very small compared with that of New York. Consequently, I interviewed only eight Korean artists in London.

The findings of my fieldwork revealed three different types of identity formation. The first type represented artists who were born outside of Korea, the second represented those who left Korea at an early age when their parents emigrated, and the third represented those who left Korea to pursue their Master of Fine Arts (MFA) after obtaining a Bachelor of Fine Arts (BFA) and then decided to settle in New York or London. In this paper, I will discuss the third type of artists' identity formation where the artists' Koreanness acts as their main roots to which new ones are added over time.

## Hong-Seon Jang: Beyond Identity Politics and Universality

Hong-Seon Jang was born in Seoul in 1971 and graduated from the Fine Art College at Dankuk University. He moved to New York in 1999 to pursue his MFA at Rochester Institute of Technology. Since then, he has been living and working in New York.

Jang's current artwork employs objects that are present in daily life. His intention is to study the quality of materials and simultaneously create three-dimensional works. For example, he made *Geographic Wave* by purchasing *National Geographic* magazines from an individual who had collected them for more than 40 years.

Figure 1. Geographic Wave.

Jang cut out each page one by one and emphasised the most important page by placing it at the front, surrounded by pages featuring events that would most likely catch the attention of the audience. Jang also intended the audience to view the work on the whole as part of natural phenomena, such as the growth of moss and mushrooms and simultaneously allow it to function as a magazine when one sees it up close. Jang cut out the shape of a mushroom from the magazine; as the mushroom sprouts from dead things like a dead tree, for Jang, it paradoxically explains the circle of life.

Figure 2. Geographic Wave detail.

For Jang, New York epitomises diversity. Jang came to New York with great excitement because he thought that more than tens of thousands of artists were gathering there to jostle with each other. As it is the case for most people, when Jang first arrived in New York, he consciously reflected on his identity. He said that when he arrived postcolonialism was the main conceptual idea in New York and that it was African Americans who frequently engaged in this discourse. Jang understood that postcolonialism resists the binary and hierarchical vision which supports Western universalism. Thus, Jang produced resistant or countercultural works dealing with his identity from the postcolonial perspective, saying to himself, "Why are only you eating? I wanna eat, too!" This social criticism was a means of resisting the dominant society. However, for Jang, such art had limitations not only in terms of the subject matter but also in terms of the medium. Jang gradually came to think of this work as overly narrow-minded. He understood that by examining one's relationships with other races and cultures, one has to consciously think about one's own identity in resisting the dominant society. So, Jang stopped doing this type of work, as he did not want to intentionally reflect (on) his Korean identity. Jang wanted his art to reflect a broader human perspective, as he thought that the latter could provide a lens through which he could see himself more precisely. Through his art, Jang wanted to seek common ground with other cultural groups. This is the reason why he used *National Geographic* as his medium because it has readers in Africa, Russia, the United States and other countries from all around the world; in essence (for Jang), everybody on the planet shares this magazine. As for the magazines' themes, Jang sees them as being easily understood universal images that depict wild life and natural phenomena.

However, one dilemma for Jang was that in pursuing universality in his art, he could not explore a discourse or an issue. For this reason, Jang's current interest is to examine his individual issues such as his implicit biases (he calls them prejudices) and their effects on shaping his identity. Jang thinks that through this process of introspection he is indirectly reflecting his own integration into American culture, as he makes more relevant contemporary artwork. As a result of this, Jang finds it difficult to classify himself (narrowly) as a Korean artist because more broadly, he considers himself to be an Oriental artist living in New York. This for Jang is important because Far East cultures share the same philosophical traditions such as Taoism, Buddhism and Confucianism.

## Sun-Kyong Kwak: Korean Roots and Contemporaneity

Sun-Kyong Kwak was born in Seoul in 1966. Kwak graduated from the Painting Department of Sookmyong University in 1992 and moved to New York in 1993 at the age of 27. Kwak graduated from New York University with an MFA. Since then, Kwak has been living and working in New York.

It is possible to characterise Kwak's artwork, which evokes Franz Kline's [6] frenetic black lines, as spontaneous line movement in the medium of black masking tape on walls. Kwak makes this kind of art (resembling performance art during the creation process), to reflect on an alternative time and space. Kwak characterised her work as "space drawing" and stated that it is a response to her surroundings in a given space. Following the image that Kwak creates, the viewers are encouraged to relate the space and time to their own bodies. Since every space is different and since no two concepts are the same, every work is different. For this reason, one can encapsulate Kwak's work as an interpretation of the essence of time and space.

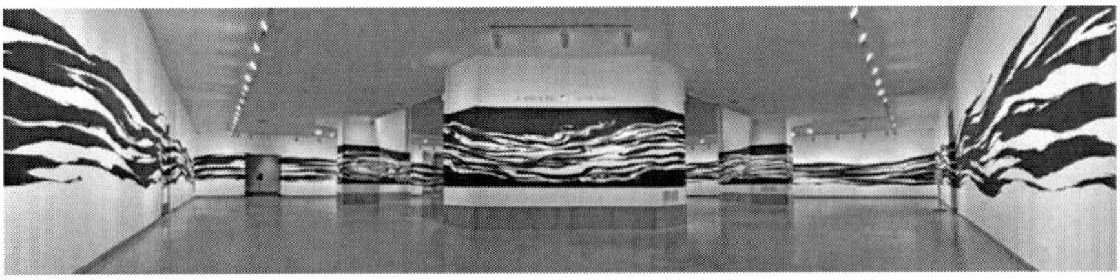

Figure 3. Unfolding 280 Hours.

Kwak's solo exhibition, *Unfolding 280 Hours* (held at the Brooklyn Museum from March to July 2009), refers to the time during which she made the artwork. When the exhibition closed, Kwak left the space empty whilst her video work faded out with the image of her tearing down the tape that was stuck to the wall. Working in the empty space, the lines grew, they faded out and then they returned to the empty space as if the artist remembered the value of 'emptiness' which was described in Chapter 11 of the ancient Taoist *Tao Te Ching* by Lao Tzu [7, 8]. For Lao Tzu, emptiness or void is the space of the idea of being and becoming. Interestingly, in this way, Kwak's empty space also reminds me of a liminal space where the empty space contained both emptiness and the memory and anticipation of life at the same time, so that the empty space becomes representative of life itself, as Homi K Bhabha in *Location of Culture* [9] (via Frantz Fanon) alludes to in his postcolonial third space. Indeed, this empty space that had been filled with life was no longer the same and suggested life as a process. Kwak was aware that her lines were comparable to life. She thereby created a new time and space that the audience could enter and experience. This invitation to experience a new space and time represents the function of her artwork. Kwak explained that her art making is "site specific," as it creates different, new narratives according to the spaces, although her medium remains the same. In other words, Kwak's idea of her masking tape is to explain the ephemeral, instant, and singular characteristic of life.

Kwak began making this masking tape art in 1995, when she was a graduate student at New York University. At the moment when the idea for using these lines struck her, she felt ecstasy and thought, "This is exactly what I wanted!" According to Kwak, her lines appear very Oriental. In Chinese art, 'line' is the most important visual element as it is thought to determine the personal qualities of the person who draws it [10]. So, to Chinese painting connoisseurs, the highest quality of line is its vividness, as it relates to the lofty nature of one's mind. Kwak's lines are reminiscent of a bold and free style which can be traced ultimately to the rough techniques of the *ip'in* (逸品) or "untrammeled" manner of Ancient T'ang and Sung painters of China [11]. Kwak was very pleased when art critics made this observation, although she has never consciously made Oriental lines. However, Kwak stated that she was drawn to Oriental lines when she was an art college student in Korea. In those days, Kwak was interested in the lines that Paul Klee [12] had executed in his paintings and the spirituality embedded in the lines of Oriental painting traditions. Although Kwak majored in Western painting, her college art curriculum did include Oriental painting classes, where she immensely enjoyed exploring the traditional techniques.

Kwak stated that her art is not only Oriental but also contemporary and if she were working on it in Korea, she could not produce such artwork. This is because her artwork is the integrated output of her encounters and experiences with other cultures. According to Kwak, whenever she moves, her art making also changes. She said that her lines have neither relation to the black and white of Franz Kline nor to Jackson Pollock's [13] action painting. Although they are similar in terms of their spontaneity, they differ in terms of their intent. For the expressionists, the main intention to explore their lines is for their self-expression, while Kwak's lines are to represent the process of instant life. The viewers' responses also differ according to the movement of the line in time and space. Kwak's intention is not for the viewers to merely see her artwork but to experience and interact with it when they are walking through the space.

When Kwak first arrived in New York, she was reluctant to reflect her Korean or Oriental identity, as she associated this identity with something being old fashioned or unrefined. However, now Kwak is content because she thinks that she reflects her Oriental identity in the most contemporary way, by embracing different spaces of other cultures in other countries and integrating them with her own culture to give birth to another hybrid life. Kwak said that others always label her as the "Korean born artist, Sun K. Kwak," as she has lived in the United States for many years. Although Kwak is satisfied with this title, she feels that she has her own unique cultural 'colour' in the multicultural city of New York where she resides.

## Jun-Gu Yoon: The Politics of Hybridisation and Translation

Jun-Gu Yoon was born in Andong, Southeastern Korea, in 1975. Yoon received his Bachelor of Arts at Keimyung University in Korea in 2000. In 2002, he moved to London, where he obtained his MA at the University of Art London in 2003, and subsequently completed his MPhil in 2009. Currently, Yoon is living and working in London as an assistant to Anthony Gormley [14], an icon of contemporary art in the United Kingdom. In 2010, Yoon published the book, *Spirituality in Contemporary Art* [15], dealing with the creation of spiritual space in art and it was shortlisted for the 2011 ACE/Mercers' International Book Award.

While Yoon used to focus on meditation from the perspective of Theravada Buddhism, his current artworks aim to change the world from the perspective of Mahayana Buddhism. Yoon's focus on the subject of money relates to this latter view. Although Theravada Buddhism and Mahayana Buddhism share the philosophy and devotion to the life and teachings of Shakyamuni Buddha, they do have some differences. Theravada Buddhism places greater emphasis on an individual's liberation whereas the aim of Mahayana Buddhism is for the salvation of the populace [16].

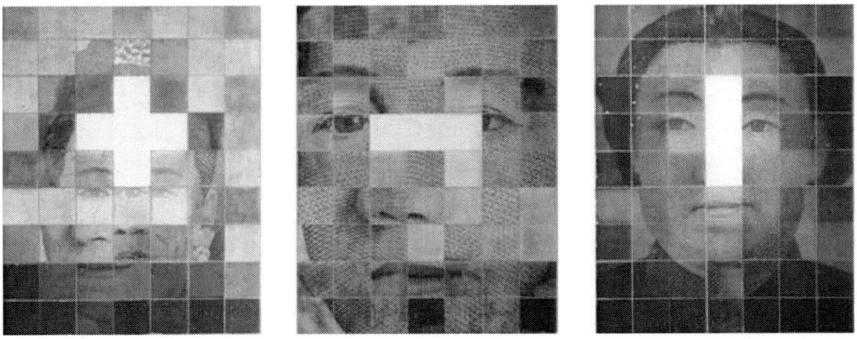

Figure 4. Heaven, Earth, Human.

At first glance, it seems paradoxical that the subject of the series is money and that Yoon uses the medium of money to discuss spirituality. *Heaven, Earth, Human* does not resemble Chinese characters but hieroglyphics. In this series, Yoon uses holes as celestial filters through which to see the world. These holes were inspired by the arrow slits or arrow loops through which arrows used to be shot in English castles. Yoon intended to represent the infinite space as suggested by the (notional) arrow flying through the celestial filter (arrow slit). This drawing-work incorporates the image of print on Korean paper, in which Yoon used ink blurring and bouncing off gold ink pigment by holding thread in his hands. Here, one can view the course of Yoon's art making as meditation. The effect of blurring, bouncing off the gold pigment, does not permit a single mistake. In short, Yoon's artistic intention was to express spirituality using a symbolic diagram of Oriental hieroglyphics.

Yoon's art emphasises "*wu* (無)" which is the most important concept in Taoist philosophy. It is usually translated as "emptiness," "void," or "nothingness." In the Taoist literature this term refers to many correlated features. For example, the void is metaphorically used to represent the symbolic aspect of one's mind that is determined by the singular thought process of the pure (re)cognition of nothingness [17]. In this context, the emptiness as an inner realisation is the very state of *Tao*. Yoon's video work, *Snow Project* [18], displays an empty road and a train with no passengers, signifying nothingness.

In another work, *Series of Bank of Heaven*, Yoon integrates figures, diagrams and letters with diverse landscapes depicting every nation's money in order to convey the idea that this is not just worldly money. Yoon's work on this project was about exploring his spirituality, as he endeavored to create a currency that one could use in Utopia by arranging every nation's sensibility, culture and thought. Although Yoon aims to achieve commercial success through mass production, like pop art, his ultimate goal is for the dissemination of spirituality. Thus, this work is distinguishable from the previous works in that it is more oriented toward the Mahayana tradition when his previous works were more focused on the Theravada teachings that mainly engaged with his personal meditation. In order to embody contemporaneity in his work, Yoon utilises modern media, such as film. However, Yoon also wants to use craftsmanship because he sees a distinction between the use of machines and that of the hand, where he believes that the latter can communicate more effectively with others.

Yoon has searched for efficient methods to make his artwork appeal to Westerners, who have a different aesthetic sensibility. Yoon thinks that Western and Oriental art differ in terms of their symbolic cultural meanings, and for this reason, Westerners tend not to properly understand his works. In his spiritual works, one method that Yoon has developed in order to give his Oriental sensitivities an appeal to western audiences, is his use of money as a medium. For Yoon, money per se is not a spiritual idea, at all, but he does consider it to be a kind of visual camouflage (or tool of obscuration). In order to attune (or align) his Oriental sensibilities and thoughts to western viewers,

Yoon thinks that the act of translation is a prerequisite and necessary procedure for his art making.

## SEARCHING FOR A THIRD SPACE

While artists like Hong-Seon Jang do not intentionally venture into identity politics, tackling racial discrimination, gender roles and ethnic issues, for most of the Korean artists that I have interviewed since 2010, identity is an ongoing process as a discourse that they develop throughout their lives. Overall, all artists consider their identity in relation to how they differ from the Other, as Stuart Hall explained in his chapter *Cultural Identity and Diaspora* [19]. When artists seek to form an identity through their art, they adopt a very dualistic approach by searching for the difference from the Other that they encounter. In this vein, each artist's journey to forge his or her own unique artistic path in the international art world (which is dominated by western aesthetics) constitutes the construction of his or her own identity in practice.

### Escaping One's Roots

During my interviews, most of the artists said that they had no compelling desire to intentionally reflect their Korean cultural identity. Since they chose a nomadic life and wanted to change when they encountered the Other, the artists wanted to be free from their roots. Therefore, they did not want to depend on the visual and mental reflexes of the Korean society in which they were born. They thought that once they were free from their roots, they could find a utopian alternative that would adequately reflect their reality in the transcultural space. For this reason, their Korean roots seemed to be an impediment to their self-transformation.

For the artists, there was a difference between their unconscious and conscious expression of their Koreanness, as they consciously resisted the stylised archetype of Koreanness. I would like to explain this using Deleuze & Guttari's [20] ideas, where searching for Koreanness consciously would mean re-territorialising identity to make a formulaic pattern. This formulaic pattern would inhibit artists from rendering a new "Body without Organs" (BwO) [21] (p. 9) in other words, a notional (underlying) body that connects both of its intrinsic and extrinsic qualities; blending the actual with the potential. A repetition of a patterned representation of Koreanness would mean 'tracing' a (mere) *reproduction* of the Korean unconscious. Judith Butler [22] would describe this 'tracing' as a performative act that creates a symbolic social sign of Koreanness. Deleuze & Guattari also advocated living a nomadic life by making a *map* rather than a '*tracing*'. For Deleuze & Guattari [23], the map is open and connectable in all of its dimensions that are oriented toward experimentation in contact with that which is Outside (real). In this vein, Nicolas Bourriaud [24] asserted that the true adversaries to creativity are neither tradition nor local cultures but confinement within formulaic cultural schemata because this is the very basis of the act of 'tracing' itself.

As Stuart Hall stated earlier, we form our identity through ambiguity and desire beyond the silence of the Other. We also form our identity on the basis of more than one discourse. The Other (in this context, the western international art world) consciously causes Korean artists to feel like entities that are unchangeable, firmly cultural, moral and geographically rooted. In this way, the Other is defined as the norm that the artists are grappling with when they are making their artworks. For the artists, it is the Other (i.e., the Western viewer) that always evokes their Koreanness. Indeed, there is a tension between seeing themselves through Western eyes and their own Korean psyches, as W.E.B du Bois [25] (p. 8) explained as "double-consciousness," where he elaborates, "[i]t is a peculiar sensation, this double-consciousness, this sense of always looking at one's self through the eyes of others." Indeed, the Korean artists in transcultural spaces have become aware through the Other's incessant requests for them to express their roots by searching for Oriental qualities whose sole purpose is for their differentiation from the Other. Whether the artists participate in solo or group exhibitions, they are always given the label "Korean-born artist," indicating that the international audience wants to treat the artists' roots as a sign of difference. On the international stage, one's roots become the *essence* of their difference. Is this really what distinguishes Koreans from the Other?

## Returning to One's Roots

Paradoxically, for the artists it was only after they had adopted the role of outsiders in order to escape their (inescapable) roots so that they could be regarded as international artists that they could actually return to their roots. It was only then that they could ask, "What is my identity?" The Korean artists had incessantly up until this point compared themselves to the Other in a dialectical position. As King Lear asks in William Shakespeare's eponymous play, "Who is it that can tell me who I am?" encountering the Other allowed the Korean artists to return to their culture (in an attempt to answer this question). Julia Kristeva [26] stated that to be able to write, one must have a distance, be both on the inside and on the outside of things. Consequently, the artists who were exiled from themselves where they were in a sense strangers to themselves could see Korean culture as a signifying system rather than as a material unconscious culture. One artist said to me:

> Up until now... we too much have sold Bhuddhas, Korean ceramics, etc. as our identity. Therefore [now] having nothing to sell... we think of those 'fixed' artifacts in museums [as no longer]... our identities. Those have no relevance to our life!

In this way, the main characteristic of expressing their Korean identity is the use of Korean metaphysical philosophy. For example, as shown in the cases of Sun-Kyong Kwak and Jun-Gu Yoon, many artists use the idea of Buddhist, Taoist, and Confucian philosophies to describe inevitable human conditions - displacement, nomadism, precarious life, death, and the like. Consequently, their subjects are more conceptual and ideal or abstract and less social and political [27] when they are visualising what a universal quality would look like for the international viewer, as Hong-Seon Jang's work tries to do.

My previous research [28] revealed that the artists' use of their Korean subject matter related to their search for a personal identity. Hence, when the artists reflected on their early lives including childhood memories, they distinguished their personal experiences in Korea from those of the Other. In other words, although the artists objected to searching for their Korean identity consciously, as they resisted being 'Korean artists' in the international arena, a Korean subject matter offered them a means to distinguish themselves from the Other *but* on their terms.

The Korean artists' return to their roots was akin to returning home after a journey and realising that it is the most comfortable place on earth. So, the inevitable destination of this journey for the artists was a return to their roots. However, the artists' roots are not the previous ones they left because they have added new lateral roots, creating a kind of dynamic collage. The artists have juxtaposed what is familiar with what they have encountered to form new creeping roots. These are no longer the roots of a tree but of a rhizome. Rhizome is the concept that Deleuze & Guattari developed to explain the multiplicity of the universe. A root-tree, with its historicity and rootedness, implies a base sequence and the process of its own generation in terms of binary logic. It represents tracing, representation, reproduction and filiation. In contrast, rhizome refers to root plants that propagate transversely, such as weeds, grass, potatoes, etc. Rhizome represents a map, an alliance, a connection and heterogeneity. It is a metaphor for multiplicity due to its fluid and non-hierarchical structure and its status of interconnected significations.

The place where the artists rhizome had arrived was located in the in-between, between oneself and the Other. This is the third space that embodies both 'Me' and the 'Other'. This psychic third space is one where neither the self nor the Other exists, it is the site where seemingly contradictory and opposite cultural elements interchange and activate in order to generate hybridity. By entering this space, the artists realised that this world of collage was made up of diverse layers of meanings. They also understood that the creation of this new space, which played a pivotal role in defining their roots, their Koreanness, was also an act of performativity, to use Judith Butler's term again. Therefore, Korean artists in transcultural spaces must constantly express their new Koreanness, (prompted by the West's othering of them) which in turn drives them to discover their rhizome roots. In a way, these roots are born out of resistance to the West's historical desire to 'master' or colonise. During this journey, the artists exist on a continuum between the two poles of escaping their Korean roots and searching for them. Consequently, they occupy a very ambiguous position; they simultaneously reject Korean culture while rediscovering it. Thus the Korean artists' encounters or interactions with the Other have led them to engage in a "double consciousness" that informs their 'double dialogue'. As such, the artists who once wanted to escape their roots have entered into a dialogue with their Koreanness to forge their own way between their roots and the corpus of aesthetic value that they have learned from modern art as the basis of contemporary international artistic inquiry. It was through this process that the artists came to see themselves as occupying a liminal position - neither me nor you.

## Liminality

The artists realised that the process of negotiating the stranger quality within themselves did not belong to a national or cultural identity. This new third space gave rise to an equally new self-created ambiguous state. Hong-Seon Jang described this clearly established process as follows:

> Still, I occasionally feel such confusion. "I am in a marginal group, I am a marginal man!" Indeed, in a way, this is neither this nor that!" Every Korean here feels this way. Now that I am here, I am forgetting the Korean language, and yet my English ability has not advanced. Therefore, I always feel foolish. I feel like that.... What makes me confused about my identity is why I, who am not White, am here now. I still feel that way. As for exhibitions, I feel the same. However, what is interesting is... I am different from foreigners. I am in-between. Thus, I am neither Korean nor American.... My work is also neither Korean nor American. Yes, I live in an obscure limbo.

It was the anthropologist Victor Turner [29] who first researched the phenomenon of liminality. According to him, in 'betwixt-and-between' liminal states, one's cultural locators become detached and then re-attached with multi-vocal symbols with many meanings. Turner (p. 27) states, "In liminality, people play with the elements of the familiar and defamiliarize them. Novelty emerges from unprecedented combinations of familiar elements."

Having established that the Korean culture is a signifying system, the artists viewed the process of expressing their Koreanness as a process of developing others forms of 'becoming' in the liminal space. Indeed, they wanted to *become* other than what was expected of them by playing with the traces of their Koreanness, which were now signifiers that they could use within their art. In this way, the idea of identity as a 'multiplicity' now had emerged. The artists' Body without Organs (BwO) as a virtual entity and as a virtual multiplicity could now be actualised in various ways. For example, they began to translate and integrate difference from the Other to form their hybrid multiplicity. This affective, virtual and multiple BwO developed into an unconscious body that overcame contradictory conflicts with the conscious body and was freed to enter unknown new dimensions along a 'line of flight.' This line had no restraints and moved forward to new possible creative domains. So, as the artists' multiplicity emerged there became no *single* clichéd actualisation of what *constituted* a Korean artist living abroad.

## Difference and Searching for the Universal

It is traditional in Oriental thought that the dynamics of difference between the *yin* and *yang* can achieve harmony beyond their extreme opposite polarities. Indeed, the artists' liminal space became a place where different cultures coexisted and where the conflict and collision between cultures generated new energy. Sun-Kyong Kwak explains this process as the following:

> Because there is something unique which comes from one's deep roots, it cannot be imitated by the Westerners, although they may want to imitate it. Therefore, we cannot catch the Western way, though we try. By the way, when one, with one's own cultural background, enters a new space, one has to embrace new cultural elements, melting one's own roots and blending them in order to make unique ones.

It is the politics of difference where there is no exclusion of this or that difference, where common ground at the level of difference can be constituted [30] According to Judith Revel [31], common ground constitutes a (quasi) 'metric' differential that is of the order of commonality or difference. For Hong-Seon Jang, to envision something universal, he searched for the common ground between cultures:

> I always try to find the common ground - people's common perspective in seeing things. Wherever you come from - Mexico, France, Japan - you should feel a common ground. This is one example. There is also memory, as everybody has memories. In everybody's memory, there is his or her own prejudice. I play the prejudice. In other words, I try to see the prejudice in a different way. To take [a] concrete example, consider furniture - it is used in every culture. There is Japanese furniture and there is German furniture. My task is to integrate them. I show the collection of every type of furniture. Indeed, there are meanings and memories in every culture to be shared.

Couze Venn [32] explained that searching for common ground is a prerequisite for recognising the hybrid characteristic of identity and culture in universality. Roland Robertson [33] offered an explanation for Jang's return to searching for his personal identity after experimenting with universality. According to Robertson, the particularisation of universalism involves the idea of the 'universal identity' being given global-human concreteness. While the universalisation of a 'personal identity' involves the extensive diffusion of an idea where there is virtually no limit to particularity, uniqueness, difference, or otherness. In this vein, Jang's search for his personal identity is also related to his exploration of universalisation.

## Translation

The course of the artists' journey to be a BwO in their liminal spaces involved the artists facilitating a dialogue between their own culture and that of the Other. When the artists saw the exchange between cultural meanings (that of their culture and that of the Other's), they understood that both were indeed equal. This eventually led the artists to the state of translation, which is the state of necessary cooperation between cultures. Julia Kristeva [34] explains that every text including a work of a poem, a painting, a work of philosophy, a scientific theory, and the like, is not the work of single author. Kristeva states that, "[a]ny text is constructed of a mosaic of quotations; any text is the absorption and transformation of another" (p. 66). This implies that a single text refers to many other texts and to the ways that symbolic systems and languages are constructed; a development of the concept of intersubjectivity with its multiple interpretations. Jun-Gu Yoon explained this act of translation as follows:

> For example, if I show "nothingness," then the English cannot understand it. Therefore, rather than talk about Oriental philosophy directly, I show the chink in the English castle. Then it is more easily understandable. Therefore, rather than talking about integrity through a Korean fine tree, I translate it into a rose, then it is more quickly understandable. Let's think of translating Korean literature into English. If translated literally, it will never touch the English-speaking audience. I utilise that point. And I am always seeking this answer. In other words, I make the Other's version.

Because translation can allow one to explain the Other's thoughts, it can facilitate a close relation with the Other. According to Bourriaud, translation is the act of transporting the object of which it lays hold, then going forth to meet the Other presenting him with the foreign in a familiar form. In this way, this connection with the Other enhances the artists' creativity as a voluntary process of double consciousness where difference becomes creative. Deleuze & Guattari posited that one can achieve creativity by interacting and connecting with others. Indeed, it is from this translation that the singularity of expression becomes possible. Consequently, the act of translation for each artist constitutes the artists' multiple hybrid identity.

## Multiple Hybrid Identity

Judith Butler [35] introduces the idea of the incessantly mobile subject, stating that there is no entity that has the same identity as another. Therefore for Emmanuel Levinas [36], real liberation is relating with the Other in such a way that one can transcend the self. Kristeva outlined a way of doing this; according to her, one constructs and deconstructs oneself, forms and reforms oneself, by intersecting with the texts of others [37] As I identified earlier, when Korean artists reject the idea of relating to the Other, they remain in a state of the root-tree as their fundamental image. However, when they accept the relation with the Other, they can reconstruct their multiple identities as rhizome.

The encounter with the Other spreads heterogeneous, multiple, secondary roots to change the main root. In this way, the artists' Koreanness is multiple, not singular in nature. It is always rediscovering, reinventing and reinterpreting. This multiplicity is not the result of consensus but of a polyphonic dialogue [38] that leads to another realm of hybrid intersubjectivity. Hong-Seon Jang explains:

> As for images now, specifically in this period, due to the Internet.... Because images are too disseminated here and there, it is impossible to absorb all. Images immediately become information - they are input in our memory. Therefore, now, cultural boundaries are increasingly blurred. There is neither mine nor yours; all are sharable. How interesting [the] image is.... Although the senses of sight and smell and an antenna or angle of contact exist, images become just information on seeing them. The sense of smell is the same - when we smell something, we distinguish that it must be that. However, an image enters directly, and then is input. This creates some prejudice. This is because of cultural differences.... Because of this intersubjectivity, the information changes. Therefore, for example, some people like my work, and some people do not like it. [Looking at] It must be a very different personal experience. Because of personal experiences, there comes personal taste. Although there must be common ground as humans, the marked difference comes from one's experience. Such differences.... I treat the division like dualism.

Deleuze & Guattari explained that short-term memory is in no way subject to a law of continuity or immediacy to its object. Since it acts at a distance, it is always under the conditions of discontinuity, rupture and multiplicity. In this way, identity, with its multiple and hybrid forms, is always 'becoming' by selection and differentiation in the process of social interaction. If culture is a way of thinking, adapting and surviving in one's environment, hybridity is a typical, noticeable characteristic of culture in the 21st century, where the world is becoming increasingly globalised. Indeed, in this century of global capitalism, diaspora and the diffusion of the Internet, diverse, contradictory and fragmentary shards of others are increasingly interconnecting to create something different, new and unrecognisable. Homi Bhabha stated that the process of creating hybridity is a result of the negotiation between meaning and representation. Therefore Yoon makes signs to imply the Other's elements in his identity, traversing seemingly incompatible forms. Not only does he arrange foreign cultural elements in his work; he also connects with the Other's meanings. Sun-Kyong Kwak explained the process of making hybridity in her artwork as follows:

> As I make this work here and another one there, as I move like this, as I move around the world, I respond to the different spaces. It is like spreading my roots here and there and blending them together. It is through jostling and blending that the possibility of these singularities can exist.

She went on to say:

> Once I thought that Koreanness [was] very much outdated, old fashioned. Therefore, I really didn't like it. By the way, I came to hear that my work is Oriental; this was not my intention at all. However, what I have achieved is to create very contemporary artwork by blending traditional Oriental qualities. In this way, my work is hybrid. Thus, whenever I travel to another country, I accept the local culture and blend it with my Oriental subject in order to give rise to another life.

Bhabha [39] explained that identification is the process of identifying with and through another object of otherness, at which point the agency of identification - the subject - is itself always ambivalent, because of the intervention of that otherness. Such hybridity that interconnection brings about reveals multiplicity and inconsistency. However, for Bhabha, the importance of hybridity is that it bears the traces of those feelings and practices that inform it, just like a translation. Therefore, hybridity causes the unsettling of meaning or discourse, as Yoon stated:

> Because the Queen appears on this money that I made, it appeals to the English. I think in this way... but I don't know whether it is true. This

is just feedback. As this is something rare for the English audience, there may be someone who disagrees. When I use this logic to communicate with the Korean audience... I don't think the Korean and Western viewers are divided in interpreting my work, because the two cultures are included, because double-sidedness exists. In other words, it becomes hybridity. That is to say, there is a perspective that a person can easily understand, but there is another perspective that person will focus on. Each one is different and can interpret my art differently.

# CONCLUSION

## Implications for Relational Multicultural Education

In this chapter, I have explored the process of differentiation and the contexts in which the artists' identity significations emerge relationally in their hybrid artworks. Indeed, my exploration of the Korean artists' practice in transcultural spaces shows that each artwork demonstrates connections with others by learning and translating from them. The artists initially perceived their Koreanness as being insufficient for allowing them to reflect contemporaneity in their artwork due to living a technologically accelerated hybrid world. In this vein, Gilbert Simondon [40] proposed that *being* is already *relational*. Furthermore, Venn [41] explained that Simondon's idea of being in a relation implies a decentering of the notion of the individual as the center for understanding the constitutions of intersubjectivity and identity.

Indeed 'being in relations' is a very traditional Oriental thought, as the basic idea of *The Avatamsaka Su'tra* (The Flower Ornament Scripture) [42] is the mutual containment and interpenetration of all phenomena. All is interrelated and interpenetrated! Just as William Blake [43, 44] could "see a world in a grain of sand," *The Avatamsaka Su'tra* explains, "In each dust-mote of these worlds are countless worlds and Bhuddhas" (p. 5). Indeed for Oriental people, Western transcendental traditions based on the works of Immanuel Kant [45] which provide a theoretical framework of an essential substance 'self' (his "Ding an sich" (thing-in-itself) (p. 115)) is not a familiar concept. From the Oriental perspective, one is in constant human and cosmic interactions. In Confucianism, one's identity is not one's independent existence. Rather, it is in one's relations to the cosmic principles, to others, to social communities and to one's own moral cultivation by which the self is brought into maturity [46].

For these reasons, understanding the relationship between the self and the Other is crucial to Confucian personal cultivation. Implying this meaning, the Chinese character for human is "人," which represents two interconnected people, as one man as "separate individual" cannot exist. The Korean developed this idea and coined the word, "人間" to refer to human as the entity that exists between peoples, which one can translate as the term, "singular plural." [47] (p. 1). Jean-Luc Nancy [48] said, "Being cannot be anything but being-with-one-another, circulating in the with and as the with of this singularity plural coexistence." (p. 3) For Venn [49], the relationality of being is acknowledging the Other within oneself in order to indicate being that is never one but is more than one. Consequently, the concept of a relational being means that our self is a constantly changing entity due to the interconnection with the Other. Therefore, the third space is the site where I and the Other transform together for "becoming" or "co-becoming."

Moreover, the relationality of being suggests that our changing identity is not a matter of the individual's autonomous decisions. It is, rather, the relational product of a process, in which the activities enacting the reality of being with others, evolve. This view rejects cultural pluralism, which has provided the theoretical framework for multiculturalism in the United States. Cultural pluralism, which emphasises distinctive, specific group identities as a construct and a creation of social material roles, relies on an essentialist ontology. The essentialist ontology takes the outcomes of a social process as the main unit of analysis. In contrast to this, relational ontology emphasises the importance of a contextualised analysis of a social process. Therefore, the relational multiculturalism that characterises relational ontology is concerned with the processes and relations that have placed a specific cultural group's value systems in a specific context. To conclude, I propose a relational multiculturalism that takes the basic units of social and cultural analysis not as individual products but as the relational process of the interaction between and among, multiple hybrid identities.

## REFERENCES


[1] DW. (2013, September 12). *More people living abroad than ever, says UN study*. Retrieved August 21, 2015, from DW: Made for Minds: http://www.dw.com/en/more-people-living-abroad-than-ever-says-un-study/a-17083834

[2] Sarup, M. (1996). *Identity Culture and the Postmodern World.* Edinburgh: Edinburgh University Press.

[3] Hall, S. (1991). Old and new identities, old and new ethnicities. In A. D. King (Ed.), *Culture, Golobalization, and the World-System* (pp. 41-68). New York: Palgrave.

[4] Bhabha, H. (1994). *The Location of Culture*. London: Routledge.

[5] Hall, S. (1996). New Ethnicities. In D. Morley, & K.-H. Chen (Eds.), *Stuart Hall: Critical Dialogues in Cultural Studies* (pp. 441 - 449). London: Routledge.

[6] MoMA. (2015, August 16). *The Collection: Franz Kline: American, 1910–1962*. Retrieved August 16, 2015, from MoMA: http://www.moma.org/collection/artists/3148

[7] Lao Tzu. (2006). *Tao Ching; Classic Chapters 1 - 37. Translated by Derek Lin.* Retrieved August 16, 2015, from Tao Te Ching: Annotated & Explained. Published by SkyLight Paths: http://www.taoism.net/ttc/complete.htm

[8] Bhabha, H. (1994). *The Location of Culture*. London: Routledge.

[9] Bush, S. (1971). *The Chinese Literati on Painting*. Cambridge, MA: Harvard University Press.

[10] Cahill, J. (1980). *An Index of Early Chinese Painters and Paintings: Tang, Sung, and Yuan.* Berkeley and Los Angeles: University of California Press.

[11] Metropolitan Museum of Art. (2000–2015). *Heilbrunn Timeline of Art History: Paul Klee (1879–1940).* Retrieved August 16, 2015, from Metropolitan Museum of Art: http://www.metmuseum.org/toah/hd/klee/hd_klee.htm

[12] TATE. (2015, August 16). *Jackson Pollock 1912–1956*. Retrieved August 16, 2015, from TATE: http://www.tate.org.uk/art/artists/jackson-pollock-1785

[13] Gormley, A. (2015, August 16). *Antony Gormley*. Retrieved August 16, 2015, from Antony Gormley: http://www.antonygormley.com/

[14] Yoon, J. (2010). *Spirituality in Contemporary Art.* London: Zidane Press

[15] Donath, D. C. (1971). *Buddhism for the West: Theravada, Mahayana and Vajrayana*. New York: The Julian Press.

[16] O'Connell, C. (2009, August 6). *Crossfields: Young Korean artists at the KCC*. Retrieved August 16, 2015, from London Korean Links: http://londonkoreanlinks.net/2009/08/06/crossfields-young-korean-artists-at-the-kcc/

[17] Hall, S. (2009). Cultural Identity and Diaspora. In J. E. Braziel and A. Mannur (Eds.), *Theorizing Diaspora* (pp. 233-246). Oxford, UK: Blackwell Publishing.
[18] Deleuze, G., & Guattari, F. (1987). *A Thousand Plateaus: Capitalism and Schizophrenia.* (B. Masumi, Trans.) Minneapolis: Minnesota University Press.
[19] Deleuze, G. & Guattari, F. (2009[1977]). *Anti-Oedipus: Capitalism and Schizophrenia.* New York, NY: Penguin Books.
[20] Boucher, G. (2006). The politics of performativity: A critique of Judith Butler. *Parrhesia*, No. 1, 112-141.
[21] Deleuze, G., & Guattari, F. (1987). *A Thousand Plateaus: Capitalism and Schizophrenia.* (B. Masumi, Trans.) Minneapolis: Minnesota University Press.
[22] Bourriaud, N. (2009). *The Radicant.* New York: Lukas & Sternberg.
[23] Du Bois, W. E. B. (2007). *The Souls of Black Folk.* Oxford: Oxford University Press.
[24] Kristeva, J. (1991). *Stranger to Ourselves.* New York: Columbia University Press.
[25] Park, J-A. (2014). Korean artists in transcultural spaces: Constructing new national identities. *International Journal of Art and Design Education*, *33* (2), 223-234.
[26] Turner, V. (1982). *From Ritual to Theatre.* New York: PAJ Publications.
[27] Venn, C. (2014). "Race" and the disorders of identity: Rethinking difference, the relation to the other and a politics of the commons. *Subjectivity*, *7* (1), 37-55.
[28] Revel, J. (2009). Identity, nature, life: Three biopolitical deconstructions. *Theory, Culture, & Society*, *26* (6), 45-54.
[29] Venn, C. (2014). "Race" and the disorders of identity: Rethinking difference, the relation to the other and a politics of the commons. *Subjectivity*, *7* (1), 37-55.
[30] Robertson, R. (1992). *Globalization.* London, Thousand Oaks, New Delhi: Sage Publications.
[31] Kristeva, J. (1980). *Desire in language: A Semiotic Approach to Literature and Art.* New York: Columbia University Press.
[32] Butler, J. (1993). *Bodies That Matter.* London: Routledge.
[33] Levinas, E. (1990). *Time and the Other.* (R. A. Cohen, Trans.) Pittsburgh, PA: Duquesne University Press.
[34] Smith, A. (1996). *Julia Kristeva: Readings of Exile and Estrangement.* Houndmills, Basingstoke, Hampshire and London: Macmillan Press Ltd.

[35] Bakhtin, M. M. (1984). *Problems of Dostoesvsky's poetics.* (C. Emerson, Trans.) Minneapolis: University of Minnesota Press.

[36] Bhabha, H. (1990). The third space: interview with Homi Bhabha by Jonathan Rutherfield. In J. Rutherfield (Ed.), *Identity, Community, Culture, Difference* (pp. 207-221). London: Lawence & Wishart.

[37] Simondon, G. (2005). *L'individuation A la Lumiere Des Notions De Forme Et D'information.* Grenoble, France: Millon.

[38] Venn, C. (2014). "Race" and the disorders of identity: Rethinking difference, the relation to the other and a politics of the commons. *Subjectivity, 7* (1), 37-55.

[39] Chang, G. C. (Ed.). (1991). *The Buddhist Teaching of Totality: The Philosophy of Hwa Yen Buddhism* (Sixth ed.). University Park, PA: The Pennsylvania State University Press.

[40] Blake, W. (2015, August 23). *Auguries of Innocence.* Retrieved August 23, 2015, from The Pickering Manuscript: http://93beast.fea.st/files/section2/blake/extras/Pickering.pdf

[41] Kant, I. (1998[1781]). *Critique of pure reason.* (P. Guyer, A. W. Wood, Eds., P. Guyer, & A. W. Wood, Trans.) Cambridge: Cambridge University Press.

[42] Yao, X-Z. (1996). Self-construction and identity: The Confucian self in relation to some Western perceptions. *Asian Philosophy*, *6*, 179-195.

[43] Nancy, J.-L. (2000). *Being Singular Plural.* (R. D. Richardson, & A. E. O'Byrne, Trans.) Stanford, CA: Standford University Press.

[44] Nancy, J.-L. (2000). *Being Singular Plural.* (R. D. Richardson, & A. E. O'Byrne, Trans.) Stanford, CA: Standford University Press.

[45] Venn, C. (2010). Individuation, relationality, affect: Rethinking the human in relation to the living. *Body & Society, 16* (1), 129-162.

# INDEX

#



A



B

## C



## D

## E



## F



## G

## H



## I



## J

## K



## L



## M

## N



## O



## P